CONSENSUS

AN ELUSIVE CONSENSUS

Nuclear Weapons and American Security after the Cold War

Janne E. Nolan

BROOKINGS INSTITUTION PRESS
Washington, D.C.

Copyright © 1999
THE BROOKINGS INSTITUTION
1775 Massachusetts Avenue, N.W., Washington, D.C. 20036
www.brookings.edu

Library of Congress Cataloging-in-Publication data

Nolan, Janne E.
An elusive consensus : nuclear weapons and American security
after the Cold War / Janne E. Nolan.
   p. cm.
   Includes bibliographical references (p.) and index.
   ISBN 0-8157-6102-3 (alk. paper)
   ISBN 0-8157-6101-5 (pbk. : alk. paper)
   1. United States—Foreign relations,1989 2. National
security—United States. 3. Nuclear weapons—Government
policy—United States. 4. Nuclear arms control—United States. 5.
Nuclear nonproliferation. I. Title.
E840.N63 1999   99-6374
327.73–dc21   CIP

9 8 7 6 5 4 3 2 1

The paper used in this publication meets minimum requirements of the
American National Standard for Information Sciences—Permanence of
Paper for Printed Library Materials: ANSI Z39.48-1984.

Typeset in Palatino

Composition by AlphaWebTech
Mechanicsville, Maryland

Printed by R. R. Donnelley and Sons
Harrisonburg, Virginia

Foreword

THIS STUDY ANALYZES the contemporary U.S. security debate by focusing on one of its core elements: the utility and missions of nuclear weapons after the cold war. The specific focus is on the attempts of the Clinton administration to define and articulate the rationale for U.S. nuclear forces absent a Soviet adversary. The study examines the political and bureaucratic dynamics of two instances of policy formulation. The first is the 1993–94 nuclear posture review, an effort to articulate a new foundation for U.S. nuclear deterrence to reflect changing strategic imperatives. The second is the debate about the role of nuclear weapons for managing regional security challenges, including the decision in 1996 to sign the African Nuclear Weapons Free Zone Treaty, which led to a stated policy reserving a U.S. right to use nuclear weapons against nonnuclear third world adversaries.

The case studies, based on extensive interviews with participants and close observers, examine the interplay between the influence of radical, contextual change—the demise of the Soviet bloc, in particular—and the way in which U.S. policymakers interpret and reflect new realities in policy initiatives and institutional arrangements. Related policy debates—including the extension of the Nuclear Non-Proliferation Treaty in 1995, the cooperative threat reduction program with Russia and other former Soviet republics, the effort to achieve international limits on nuclear testing, and the debate over the desirability of missile defenses—

also are discussed as they relate to the two main cases. The focus, however, is on the evolution of U.S. nuclear strategy.

The post–cold war nuclear debate lacks the overt partisan tensions and public passions of the past. Discussions of strategic nuclear weapons seem strangely passé even among many security experts, a throwback to a distant reality or the arcane preoccupation of specialists reluctant to turn to more pressing problems. The debate about the direction of U.S. nuclear policy is nonetheless still a significant factor in the U.S. security debate. Fundamental divisions remain among policymakers and experts over the role and importance of nuclear weapons for deterring past adversaries, including Russia and China, for extending deterrence to long-standing allies in Europe and Asia, for projecting deterrence globally against states well beyond traditional U.S. security perimeters, and increasingly, for dissuading or coercing states from acquiring or using nuclear, chemical, or biological weapons.

This discussion of nuclear weapons policy is a microcosm of broader issues of American adaptation to a new international system. The design of security policies that can preserve U.S. global leadership and advance U.S. interests depends not only on the character and receptivity of the international environment, but also on domestic politics. A successful U.S. transition to a post–cold war world will depend on forging an enduring domestic security consensus, a challenge that is proving to be more difficult than was widely anticipated just a few years ago. The articulation of publicly compelling post–cold war policies is hindered not only by the greater complexity of security challenges, but also by the process of domestic adaptation to policies that may challenge the familiar orthodoxies and institutional arrangements that preserved the national security consensus for more than four decades.

The author would like to thank the many individuals inside and outside government who gave generously of their time and expertise to advance this research. A list of the people who assisted in this project would be far too long. Some who deserve special thanks, however, are the author's former colleagues at Brookings, including Charlotte Baldwin, Bruce Blair, Yahya Sadowski, John Steinbruner, and Mark Strauss, and three who reviewed the manuscript in draft form, including Richard Betts, Michael Nacht, and Larry Welch. The author also acknowledges Richard Haass, director of foreign policy studies, for his endurance as this project evolved. A number of critical sources, especially senior government officials, have asked to remain anonymous;

they were nevertheless invaluable in providing insight into evolving policy decisions.

The manuscript could not have been completed without the assistance of Bridget Butkevich, Susan Jackson, Stacy Knobler, Jim Ludes, Rebecca Over, Farid Senzai, Louise Skillings, Andrew Solomon, and Christina Woodward. At the Brookings Institution Press, Diane Hammond edited the manuscript, Joanne Lockhard proofread the pages, and Robert Elwood provided the index under the direction of Janet Walker. The author also thanks the John D. and Catherine T. MacArthur Foundation and the Carnegie Corporation for their generous financial support.

The views expressed in this book are solely those of the author and should not be attributed to the Brookings Institution, to its trustees, officers, or other staff members, or to the organizations that support its research.

Michael H. Armacost
President

June 1999
Washington, D.C.

Contents

CHAPTER ONE

Introduction

THE TRANSFORMATION OF THE international environment in recent years has challenged the orthodoxies that guided U.S. security policy during the cold war. The international system heralded by President George Bush as the new world order in 1991 rested on the idea of significantly reduced international tensions. The material threat of concerted military aggression against the United States and its allies by an equal or superior adversary ceased to be a dominant public preoccupation. Former communist adversaries became recipients of Western assistance in their transition to democracy and market economies, and three have since become members of the North Atlantic Treaty Organization. In addition, an ambitious program to denuclearize three former Soviet republics (Kazakhstan, Belarus, and Ukraine) has been largely successful.

Multiple initiatives undertaken by the Bush administration and since supported by the administration of President Bill Clinton have moved to reduce the size of U.S. and Russian nuclear arsenals, to withdraw nuclear weapons from the battlefield and from most naval vessels, to take strategic bombers off alert, to cease nuclear testing, and to seek an international halt to the production of weapons-related fissile materials (see chapter 2). Whereas once the United States viewed Russia's conventional forces as capable of defeating the Western alliance, the United States now sees a state that could not successfully suppress a separatist insurgency on its own territory. As Admiral Henry G. Chiles, former commander of the U.S. Strategic Command (STRATCOM), summarizes it: "The Cold War is over. The strategic confrontation between the United States and the Soviet Union has been replaced by a fundamentally new relationship with a different set of countries based on cooperative threat reduction and mutual downsizing of strategic forces."[1]

That said, it is now a cliché in Washington that the end of the ideological struggle with the Soviet Union was not necessarily good news. A predictable bipolar system, according to this view, has been replaced by the threat of global uncertainty—a world of complexity that makes the Soviet Union seem simple and manageable by comparison. Nor has the dissolution of the cold war paradigm, with its central focus on the antagonism between two rival superpowers, ushered in an era of domestic euphoria. Far from it. "We have slain the dragon," says James Woolsey, former director of the Central Intelligence Agency, "but we live now in a jungle filled with a bewildering variety of poisonous snakes."[2]

The relative optimism expressed in the latter part of the Bush administration about the promises of the post–cold war era seem to have been progressively overshadowed by a heightened sense of urgency about how the United States will cope with new or more complicated threats. The evolved, articulated codes of conduct and rules of engagement between the United States and its principal adversary are no longer a reliable foundation for security. Secretary of Defense William Cohen says that "as the new millenium approaches, the United States faces a heightened prospect that regional agressors, third-rate armies, terrorist cells, and even religious cults will wield disproportionate power by using . . . nuclear, biological, or chemical weapons against our troops in the field and our people at home. . . . Indeed, a paradox of the new strategic environment is that American military superiority actually *increases* the threat . . . by creating incentives for adversaries to challenge us asymmetrically."[3]

Nearly ten years after the fall of the Berlin Wall, policymakers and experts struggle still to articulate an alternative catchword for U.S. involvement in this bewildering environment. What is the modern analogue of containment? Where is the brilliant Generation X "Mr. X"who will solve this dilemma? The United States needs a new set of legitimating beliefs and institutional arrangements to justify U.S. involvement in international problems, ranging from preventing Russian internal collapse to projecting force on the Korean peninsula—challenges that do not fit the standard definitions of intervention. The difficulties emerge in trying to reconcile popular and deep-seated conceptions of U.S. power with security challenges that require more complicated instruments. There is a vast difference between decisive technological supremacy over a coherent enemy and instruments that will prevent the spread of lethal biological agents, target terrorist organizations, or deploy troops to defuse instabilities or to counter unconventional means of warfare.[4]

Several official and quasi-official studies of the recent past highlight the degree to which the United States is unprepared for these new challenges. A report prepared by the Defense Science Board in October 1997, for example, argues that the Pentagon has yet to seriously address "the unconventional, or asymmetric, threats military planners and defense experts believe pose some of the greatest hazards to U.S. national security."[5] The United States' halting and difficult adjustment is obvious, but the reasons for it are not well understood. Some think that the Clinton administration's lack of leadership is to blame. Others see it as the result of a "natural" time lag in the process of adaptation to a new set of circumstances. Or it is said to be simply a reflection of the constraints imposed by the American public's disinterest in international affairs.[6]

While these explanations have validity, there are deeper and more interesting factors to be examined. These have to do with the organization of U.S. institutions established during the cold war, the belief systems that have sustained an enduring consensus about national security, and the ways in which the system has coped, and continues to cope, with the need to protect authority for national security in a world in which public support of vital missions may no longer be ensured. The abrupt political changes brought about by the dissolution of the Soviet Union, in other words, pose challenges to the U.S. political system reminiscent of dilemmas described in Thomas Kuhn's *The Structure of Scientific Revolutions*, in which the disintegration of a central paradigm forces a sudden and unexpected reexamination of the motivating assumptions and organizational arrangements that have defined national objectives for almost a half a century.[7]

This study analyzes the contemporary U.S. security debate by focusing on one of its core elements: the utility and missions of nuclear weapons after the cold war. The specific focus is on the experiences of the Clinton administration in trying to define and articulate the rationale for U.S. nuclear forces absent a Soviet adversary. The study examines the political and bureaucratic dynamics of two instances of policy for-

3

mulation. The first is the 1993–94 Nuclear Posture Review, an effort to articulate a new foundation for U.S. nuclear deterrence to reflect changing strategic imperatives. The second is the debate about the role of nuclear weapons for managing regional security challenges, including the decision in 1996 to sign the Africa Nuclear Weapons–Free Zone Treaty, which led to a stated policy reserving the U.S. right to use nuclear weapons against nonnuclear third world adversaries.

The case studies examine the interplay between the influence of radical, exogenous change—the demise of the Soviet bloc, in particular—and the way in which U.S. policymakers interpret and reflect new realities in policy initiatives and institutional arrangements. Related policy debates—including, inter alia, the extension of the Nuclear Non-Proliferation Treaty in 1995, the cooperative threat reduction program with Russia and other former Soviet republics, the effort to achieve international limits on nuclear testing, and the debate over the desirability of missile defenses—also are discussed as they relate to the two main cases. The focus, however, is on the evolution of U.S. nuclear strategy. Although pertinent, a detailed examination of related policy struggles—including the debate over missile defense or the Comprehensive Test Ban—is beyond the scope of this study.

The design of security policies that can preserve U.S. global leadership and advance U.S. interests depends not only on the character and receptivity of the international environment but also on domestic politics. A successful U.S. transition to a post–cold war world will depend on forging an enduring domestic consensus, a challenge that is proving to be more intractable than was widely anticipated just a few years ago. The articulation of publicly compelling post–cold war policies is hindered not only by the greater complexity of security challenges but also by the process of domestic adaptation to policies that may challenge the familiar orthodoxies and institutional arrangements that preserved the national security consensus for more than four decades.

The post–cold war nuclear debate lacks the overt partisan tensions and public passions of the past. The end of the superpower nuclear rivalry seems to be an accepted reality among broad elements of the public and the media, and the threat of strategic nuclear war seems to be practically nonexistent in the public consciousness. Discussions of strategic nuclear weapons seem strangely passé even among many security experts, a throwback to a distant reality or the arcane preoccupation of specialists reluctant to turn to more pressing problems. As one

Clinton administration official puts it, "On the worry list, arms control comes in somewhere between the strength of the Mexican peso and the fight against drugs."[8] There is a general perception that post–cold war nuclear arsenals are smaller, and their role is deemphasized accordingly. In the public mind, nuclear weapons are considered increasingly to be weapons of terrorism for lawless states or criminals, not a central priority, let alone a basis for calculated aggression, for the great powers. As indicated in public opinion data, a large majority of Americans now think of nuclear dangers in terms of potential threats posed by terrorists or irrational rogue leaders.[9]

The debate about the direction of U.S. nuclear policy is nonetheless still a significant factor in the U.S. security debate. Fundamental divisions remain among policymakers and experts over the role and importance of nuclear weapons for deterring past adversaries, including Russia and China, for extending deterrence to long-standing allies in Europe and Asia, for projecting deterrence globally against states well beyond traditional U.S. security perimeters, and increasingly, for dissuading or coercing states from acquiring or using nuclear, chemical, or biological weapons. The significant force-level changes implemented in recent years have not resolved fundamental dilemmas about the potential roles and missions of nuclear weapons, both as responses to emerging global challenges and as distinctly new threats to the United States.

The Purpose of the Study

To illustrate these policy dilemmas and how they are being addressed, this study develops detailed narratives of two sets of policy deliberations based on extensive interviews with participants and close observers. In addition to describing how these debates evolved, the purpose is to explore how and to what degree domestic political factors—including presidential leadership, bureaucratic disputes, congressional opinion, protection of institutional prerogatives, and the advice of private experts—influenced the outcome of national security decisions. The fundamental question has to do with how political consensus in support of national security is being formed after the cold war.

The case studies illustrate a policy process involving protracted bureaucratic and partisan conflict in which the difficulties of reconciling

5

competing views among the individuals and agencies involved supplant or significantly modify the original goal of achieving a stated alteration in national policy. Despite a perceived need by leaders to accommodate changed security circumstances, policy initiatives are quickly deflected by competition among rival agencies to retain traditional missions and rationales, fueled by political influences in the Congress and in the private sector. The resulting policy decisions reflect complex compromises among competing factions, which for the most part ratify existing policies as a way to defuse controversies over alternatives.

These phenomena are not new, nor are they unique to the cases under consideration. Understanding the way in which key decisions are formed, by whom, and to what end, however, helps demonstrate the process of U.S. adaptation after the cold war. The objective is not to recommend either an abrupt break with the past or a set of radically new proposals. The focus is on the evolving policy process and how it affects the latitude of senior leadership to make critical choices for future security. Although it is customary in studies of nuclear strategy to advance proposals for different force postures, such analyses are rarely concerned with the factors that affect the implementation of change, radical or otherwise. This study is focused on the process of decisionmaking, which any major innovation would have to take into account.

Domestic Politics, International Policies

Even casual observers of national security policy formulation understand that bureaucratic and political conflict, whether it originates in the inter- and intra-agency executive branch context, between the executive branch and the Congress, or more diffusely between governmental and outside interest groups, is endemic in policymaking.[10] Different organizations and decisionmakers, it is obvious, represent certain biases and act in particular ways to advance those biases, some more powerfully than others. Each key national security agency developed during the cold war—from the National Security Council, to the civilian leaders of the State and Defense Departments, to the Joint Chiefs and their subordinate commands—brings perspectives to the table that reflect distinct institutional origins, mandates, and agendas. Leadership in a dynamic democratic system is defined at its core as the ability to adjudicate conflicting views and to supersede parochialism in order to design coherent policies that reflect the national interest. Competing political interests and bureaucratic agendas may make it difficult to arrive at optimum solutions, but they also make it difficult for a minority opinion to undertake policies that reflect narrow or misguided interests.

Domestic divisiveness over foreign policy has ebbed and flowed over time but has many precedents, particularly in periods in which international conditions have changed markedly. In a 1984 book by I. M. Destler, Leslie H. Gelb, and Anthony Lake, for example, the authors conclude, "For two decades, the making of American foreign policy has been growing far more political—or more precisely, far more partisan and ideological. The White House has succumbed, as former Secretary of State Alexander Haig . . . put it, to 'the impulse to view the presidency as a public relations opportunity and to regard Government as a campaign for reelection.' And in less exalted locations, we Americans—politicians and experts alike—have been spending more time, energy and passion in fighting ourselves than we have in trying, as a nation, to understand and deal with a rapidly changing world."[11]

The trend toward domestic politicization of foreign policy sets the broader context for the issues being examined in this study. One difference is that past debates were conducted when the basic framework for U.S. security defined by the primacy of the Soviet threat was not seriously in question. In the current climate, uncertainty about the future has sparked pointed debate about security interests and policy options that tests the ability of policymakers to preserve consensus. Defining the basis for U.S. nuclear security is more complex, and the policy process often more adversarial, in the absence of commonly accepted interpretations of international threats and appropriate instruments. The management of domestic divisions, accordingly, is an increasingly important determinant of policy choices. Representative Curt Weldon (R-Pa.) says that "we have allowed ourselves to become polarized as policy-makers. We have a group of people that wants to re-create Russia as the evil empire, and they largely exist in my party. That's totally wrong. I don't for a minute think that Boris Yeltsin or his senior advisers want an all-out attack on America. I think that's the farthest thing from their mind. But on the other hand, we have the more liberal elements in the Congress, and that's typically the other party, who want to deny reality. . . . [They] think that by signing a few pieces of paper, that will resolve all the problems."[12]

In both of the case studies, the clash of views among midlevel officials and the effort to deflect political opposition from critics in the Congress or public narrow the choices available to senior leaders to marginal modifications of existing policies. Even if "the only constant is change," as the new Pentagon axiom puts it, choosing policies that refer back to the premises and practices of the past seems critical in eliciting consensus. These dynamics have been clearly evident in other areas of policy deliberations, including the Clinton administration's efforts to conduct comprehensive reviews of defense priorities in the 1993 Bottom-Up Review and the congressionally mandated Quadrennial Defense Review in early 1997. Although initiated to reorient U.S. defense priorities in light of changed security circumstances, both studies essentially reaffirmed existing force levels, defense programs, and budgetary priorities, albeit with reference to the new demands of a changed security environment. Both reviews have been widely criticized for their lack of vision.[13] These criticisms ignore the systemic constraints on visionary analysis in a process that relies on bureaucratic consensus to set the parameters of the debate—a direct parallel to the cases under consideration here.[14]

Democracy and Delegated Authority

The difficulties in forging a consensus for a post–cold war nuclear agenda raise questions about the role of presidential leadership, the importance of institutional self-preservation, and the level of influence exerted by advocates of different points of view in the executive branch, the Congress, and the private sector. The quest for a new consensus also raises some critical questions about the management of national security in U.S. democracy. Examining the delegation of authority to craft nuclear security policies illuminates how and why the process of adjustment may test fundamentally important elements of U.S. institutions.[15]

The U.S. government is uniquely designed to protect against the concentration and abuse of power. The founding fathers established an elaborate system of checks and balances, with the sanctity of this principle in mind. An open democratic system, however, makes it inherently difficult to shape coherent policies based on widespread public participation, especially in areas that require complex judgments and expertise, such as nuclear security. One way to resolve the tension between democratic processes and the need for stable security arrangements is to grant significant authority to institutions that can be protected from systematic disruption by external influence, including the vagaries of partisan politics and public sentiment. This is particularly (although not uniquely) the case for matters involving not only a high level of technical expertise but also access to information that is restricted even among policymakers and elected officials.[16] Throughout the cold war, a system of "guardianship," articulately described by Robert Dahl, worked effectively to delegate day-to-day authority for nuclear plans and operations to a relatively small number of civilian and military officials.[17] Guidance provided by political authorities to nuclear planners is within the purview of very few individuals; and nuclear targeting and attack planning has evolved over time into a highly specialized occupation based on specific skills, computer models, and data bases, which limit the field of expertise to only a very few.

Domestic policy—from taxation to fiscal policy—also requires complex expertise and a delegation of decisions to expert judgment. The key difference between these concerns and nuclear planning is the more limited role of both interest groups and elected officials in discussions about nuclear operations, for reasons of secrecy as well as of complexity, to say nothing of the stakes involved in the management of nuclear forces. This is not to suggest that disagreements never arise in the planning of nuclear operations or in selecting nuclear requirements. It is rather to emphasize that participation in such discussions is circumscribed and, notwithstanding discussions about details of the plans (such as targeting priorities, which have shifted over time), that the core rationales guiding these plans have not been subject to wide debate. There is, however, an important distinction between authority for setting nuclear policy—defining the broad outlines of nuclear strategy or conducting arms control negotiations, for example, which typically involve a wider array of participants—and authority for operational policy—the procedures, organizations, and instruments used in planning nuclear operations, or what some call command authority.[18]

This system depends on the tacit acquiescence of the public and elected officials to the superior expertise and authority of professionals to determine the content and character of nuclear plans. Such acquienscence effectively deflects excess interference from the outside and, moreover, discourages internal divisiveness. The demands for unfailing loyalty and cohesiveness among officials charged with managing and executing war plans distinguish nuclear operations from other areas of public policy. Russell Dougherty, commander of the Strategic Air Command in the 1970s, describes an incident in which a Minuteman missile control officer expressed some hesitation in a training exercise about whether he would "turn keys" in response to orders to launch missiles. As the commander remembers it, the officer answered, "Yes, he would turn keys upon receipt of an authentic order from proper authority; if he thought the order was legal; if he thought the circumstances necessitated an ICBM [intercontinental ballistic missile] launch; if he was convinced that it was a rational, moral necessity." In what was to become a highly publicized and controversial decision, Dougherty dismissed the officer from the air force. Dougherty drew a sharp distinction between public perceptions of responsibility, which may accept the legitimacy of individual dissent based on conscience, and the kind of discipline needed to ensure nuclear security: "The U.S. military has no place for officers, noncommissioned officers or other enlisted persons who apply their own subjective conditions to the decision to act on a valid order from proper authority."[19]

Efforts by appointed officials to become involved in operational issues also illustrate the degree to which intrusion into this area of decisionmaking is discouraged and often unsuccessful. Richard Stillwell, a deputy to Fred Ikle, undersecretary of defense for policy in the Reagan administration, drafted guidance that included precise directives about nuclear targeting, including details about how and where to allocate weapons to specific targets. The draft was part of an ongoing effort by political appointees and career professionals, including Frank Miller (currently the acting assistant secretary of defense for international security and policy), to impose higher levels of political oversight and to force greater flexibility in targeting plans. The response from General Jack Merritt, then director of the Joint Chiefs, is forthright: "Penny ante civilian bureaucrats getting involved," he says. "It was full of targeting packages, options, how to do targeting, even where and when to launch. It was all just done in the interest of imposing bureaucratic will. We got it much abbreviated, to get at least some of the baloney out." Merritt continues: "You start talking about targeting or strategic command and control and, baby, that's the family jewels. Anyone outside the uniformed military who tried this, the Chiefs told them to jump in the lake."[20] Such episodes provide insight into the political complexities of managing nuclear operations, an area of long-standing tension between professionals and "outsiders." These are not turf battles, at least not exclusively. As Dougherty argues, signs of discord in the national command authority about nuclear objectives could threaten national cohesion, whose preservation "may depend critically on keeping the fact of such debate from the public."[21]

During the cold war, decisionmakers were not called upon by the Congress or the public to articulate clear guidelines about what should be targeted, for what reason, with what level of destructive force, or for what specific political and military objective. Decisions by elected officials about funding for nuclear weapons were then, as now, not linked systematically to empirical judgments about what was needed to achieve deterrence or even to carry out official targeting policy. Few ever questioned why exactly one hundred M-X missiles or exactly one hundred B-1 bombers were required, not more or less, to uphold operational requirements, which few elected officials understand. As Louis Henkin notes, "When Congress appropriates funds for particular weapons, it acquiesces in the strategy which those weapons imply."[22] Deference to professional judgments in such matters may be appropriate, but the lack of interest or active involvement among elected officials inhibits informed discourse and the responsibility for oversight required by the Constitution.

The assumptions and criteria guiding the planning of nuclear operations remain among the most closely guarded areas in U.S. defense policy. Comprehensive concepts such as containment and deterrence served as immensely flexible rationales for a variety of security objectives, which, especially in the nuclear arena, could be pursued with a minimum of controversy. Although subject to periodic outbursts of elite and public criticism of specific policies, the debate about nuclear weapons never posed a significant challenge to the rationales and planning priorities underlying nuclear weapons development, force structures, and overall strategy. The threat of virtual annihilation by a determined and at least equal Soviet adversary was not in dispute. The need to deter massive Soviet aggression against allies in NATO or Asia, including the initiation of nuclear weapons in conflicts that could escalate to strategic confrontation, was largely an accepted tenet of Western survival.

The need to maintain forces for "parity," "essential equivalence," "escalation dominance," or other technical-numerical renderings of the struggle to deny the Soviet Union perceived advantages from military aggression confined debates about the desirable expansion or modernization of the U.S. nuclear posture to details, not core assumptions. The exceptions have been limited and largely irrelevant in influencing policy, including normative objections to nuclear war plans, such as the 1983 pastoral letter of the U.S. Catholic bishops, questions about the legality of nuclear arsenals (most recently the 1996 advisory opinion of the International Court of Justice claiming that the legal status of nuclear weapons is in question in light of the obligations undertaken as part of article 6 of the Nuclear Non-Proliferation Treaty), and the ongoing opposition to nuclear weapons by pacifist groups and disarmament lobbies.[23] One could also argue that President Ronald Reagan's 1983 vision for a strategic defense initiative challenging the core assumptions of nuclear deterrence based on "mutual assured destruction (MAD)," which he repeatedly decried as morally bankrupt, was equally ineffectual.

The Current Debate

Since the early 1990s, negotiated arsenal reductions and a host of accompanying initiatives aimed at halting the U.S.-Russian nuclear competition have imposed changes in nuclear policy, including nuclear operations. Bombers are no longer on alert, and missiles have been detargeted away from Russian territory, albeit as a symbolic measure that is readily reversible. (The agreement reached in May 1994 between the United States and Russia retargeted ballistic missiles toward the Arctic Ocean, but neither side has been interested in undertaking steps, such as changing the target sets programmed in the missiles' computer memories, that would obviate the ability to retarget the missiles in a matter of minutes.)[24] Formal guidance adopted during the Reagan administration calling for the ability of U.S. nuclear forces to "prevail even under the condition of a prolonged war" similarly has been amended— for the first time since 1981. This guidance now states that forces are for "deterring nuclear wars or the use of nuclear weapons at any level, not fighting with them."[25]

The notion of prevailing in a nuclear war was widely considered a chimerical mission even with massive nuclear forces, but this criticism became more pointed by the reductions in forces envisioned in the arms control agreements initiated by the Bush administration. The change in the formal guidance reportedly was prompted by General Eugene Habiger, commander of STRATCOM, and General John Shalikashvili, chairman of the Joint Chiefs, who informed the president in February 1996 that existing directives for nuclear strategy could not be implemented with the force level of 3,000–3,500 weapons envisioned under the Strategic Arms Reduction Treaty (START) II, which was signed by Bush in 1992.[26] As articulated by Robert Bell, senior director for defense policy and arms control in the Clinton administration's National Security Council, the new guidance shifts the emphasis from winning a nuclear conflict to deterring a nuclear conflict, although it does not alter existing requirements to be prepared to launch large- or small-scale nuclear strikes in response to a warning of a nuclear attack. The directive also retains the option of initiating the use of nuclear weapons against aggressors—now modified to include nonnuclear nations that have "prospective access" to nuclear capabilities.[27]

As the deliberations over recent guidance suggest, changes in the strategic nuclear force posture of recent years have been accepted and implemented in a way that ensures continuity in the basic construct of nuclear strategy. Streamlined target lists reflect the decline in the number of Russian and former Soviet forces and installations, while planners develop new types of targeting against emerging "rogue" states. These modifications notwithstanding, the objective that has informed strategy for more than four decades—to target Russian command centers and nuclear forces with high levels of damage expectancy—remains intact. The nuclear posture ratified by the Clinton administration is consistent with that of his predecessors and is predicated on the belief that "many thousands of targets must be held at risk with nuclear warheads to achieve deterrence."[28] As Admiral Chiles put it: "Our mission reflects continuity with the past: to deter major military attack against the United States and its allies and, if attacked, to employ forces."[29]

An Elusive Consensus

The cold war nuclear consensus was not easily achieved and may be even harder to relinquish. In the absence of a widely accepted and coherent nuclear threat and new challenges on the horizon, it is proving difficult to advance clearer or different rationales to guide future nuclear missions. An active debate among security specialists is under way. Some of these discussions are beginning to touch on what long have been considered taboo or far too arcane subjects: questioning the logic that drives the targeting and alert status of the force posture, for example, or questioning whether a triad of strategic forces maintained in a high state of readiness is even necessary in light of new security circumstances. Establishment organizations like the Council on Foreign Relations and the National Academy of Sciences have undertaken studies of whether the United States could consider the objective of global elimination of nuclear weapons.[30] The many issues under consideration include the potential for substituting advanced conventional weapons for nuclear forces, the role of nuclear weapons to deter nonnuclear states that possess chemical or biological weapons, and whether the United States should abrogate the Anti-Ballistic Missile Treaty in favor of immediate deployment of national missile defenses.[31]

Opinion about alternative options is widely divided, but the ongoing debate is qualitatively different from its cold war predecessors. It is no longer exclusively the purview of specialists or activists with singular agendas. Former officials, senior military officers, and recognized defense experts, including conservatives who manned the ramparts of the cold war, are involved in detailed studies that intrude on issues of operational sensitivity. In perhaps the most dramatic example, General George Lee Butler, former STRATCOM commander, began in 1996 to publicly question the safety and wisdom of nuclear operations, highlighting instances in which accidents or mistakes posed severe risks to Americans. The excoriation of nuclear weapons by a former nuclear commander in chief has no clear precedent. Many question his judgment, but no one can dispute his extensive expertise.[32]

Whether and how these discussions will affect internal policy formulation is yet to be fully revealed. Key questions, however, are whether nuclear planning and the formation of strategy will continue to rely on a system of closely guarded authority or, conversely, whether the quest for a new consensus will impose greater openness in a way that could intrude on current institutional alignments. An editorial in the *Washington Post* criticizes the Clinton administration for attempting to amend nuclear guidance in secret: "Mr. Clinton made this latest nuclear policy decision behind closed doors. No doubt that's easier. But he loses the public understanding and support that could flow from an open process. 'Rocket science' has become a metaphor for intellectual challenge, but rocket science in the sense of nuclear policy has shown itself to be well within the perimeter of public discussion. Mr. Clinton owes the public—where is Congress, anyway?—a nuclear word."[33] This is a distinct departure from what has long been a fairly constrained discussion among elites. The idea of more open deliberations about nuclear plans may be misguided or illusionary; it is certainly heretical for those who are directly involved. Public discussion of plans for nuclear operations has been carefully, if not always successfully, avoided. This is one reason that a formal distinction was made among the four elements of strategic doctrine, separating declaratory policy—what is said publicly—from the employment, acquisition, and deployment policies that make up the actual plans for nuclear operations.

The increased scrutiny of the premises of nuclear policy, however, may be inevitable. The arms control initiatives of recent years have been initiated and concluded without the laborious negotiations of the past and have been conducted in relatively open discussions among senior political leaders. Consideration of new nuclear options for third world aggressors, in turn, has prompted media commentary and may prompt wider debate as new policies are implemented. The rise of new nuclear risks, especially terrorism, also has captured public attention, including Hollywood thrillers. A poll of 800 registered voters in September 1997, for example, elicited responses about issues such as de-alerting nuclear forces (favored by 66 percent), increasing security at nuclear sites (favored by more than 80 percent), assisting with the dismantling of weapons in Russia (favored by more than 80 percent), and reducing all nations' arsenals to a few hundred (favored by more than 66 percent). Results of public opinion polls are obviously imprecise, and answers vary according to the way questions are asked. It is still unusual by cold war standards to engage the public at this level of technical detail.[34]

The heightened interest in nuclear dangers may pose implications not just for the rationale that has long guided nuclear planning but, as suggested, for the way in which authority is delegated. The unique status accorded to the nuclear command and its cadre of civilian overseers, along with the high degree of secrecy and complex expertise needed to plan nuclear operations, creates distinct disincentives to widen participation—to say nothing of the sensitivity of public reactions to discussions of nuclear war plans. The most recent revision of the guidance, for example, was carefully protected among a handful of indi-

viduals, deliberately excluding agencies and individuals with responsibility for nuclear policy, including the Department of Energy and senior arms control officials in the Department of State.[35]

A key question for this study is how the institutions and individuals
currently responsible for nuclear operations will calibrate pressure for
a new consensus with the need to devise policies that involve highly
sensitive decisions and activities. Judging from the case studies, this
challenge will require extremely careful management. Whether or how
systemic changes in institutional arrangements may be considered and
implemented will in part depend on the receptivity of professionals
who have been involved in the day-to-day management of nuclear
matters. In an interview in early 1997, General Habiger may have anticipated challenges of this kind when, in response to the question, If
there is a START III, what would you like to see it address? he answered,
"Number one, that as responsible Commander in Chief, I get to play in
that process."[36] Conversely, it will depend on the degree to which the
desire to maintain current arrangements conflicts with desired policy
changes in ways that leaders may not fully appreciate.

The resistance of institutions to certain innovations is a well-
documented phenomenon in public policy.[37] The degree to which it may
influence or limit national choices in the national security sphere, however, is not well understood. Efforts to expose sensitive areas of
decisionmaking to higher levels of public scrutiny goes to the heart of a
dilemma posed by Dahl about the nature of democracy: "That decisions on nuclear strategy and other complex issues are made by the few
rather than the many—quite likely even by the meritorious few—is not
simply a consequence of an effort to prevent discussion and participation by a broader and more representative selection of the *demos*, though
that may be part of the explanation. If only that were true, however,
solutions would be much easier to suggest. But it is instead mainly a
consequence of the fact that the democratic process is not equipped to
deal with questions of exceptional complexity."[38]

Can a new consensus be formed and protected without some system
of guardianship? Can this be achieved in a manner that avoids protracted controversies, which can be divisive to the body politic? The
doctrinal, political, and bureaucratic conflicts sparked by the 1993–94
Nuclear Posture Review are by no means inevitable, but they are at
least informative about the tensions and divisions to be avoided. As
General Butler noted in 1992, "What matters now is the manner in which

victory [in the cold war] is consolidated, the orderly quest for a new paradigm, the patient reconstruction of consensus, the intelligent transition from old postures into new, and the preservation of an environment which will continue to attract and retain a quality force of volunteers."[39] His invocation for patience and orderly evolution may strike Butler's critics as ironic in light of his call for the abolition of nuclear forces in 1996; his description of the challenges, however, rings no less true.[40]

The Scope of Book

Chapter 2 provides an overview of the political-military context in which the new Clinton administration undertook efforts to craft U.S. nuclear policy for the post–cold war era, setting the stage for the two case studies. The determination of the Bush administration to recast the foundations of nuclear security proved under Clinton to be highly constrained by domestic divisions both about the desirability of change and about the correct interpretation of external events.

Chapters 3 and 4 present the case studies. Both are based on primary sources and, in almost all cases, interviews with participants. The objective is to provide a narrative analysis of decisionmaking as it actually took place, revealing the competing perspectives, power alignments, and interests that fought the policy battles and that, ultimately, account for the policy outcomes. The episodes under examination are very recent, and they contain elements of continuing debates. Due to the sensitivity of the decisions and the real-time nature of the process, many sources have asked to remain anonymous. The depiction of events contained in the cases are based on the corroboration of at least two or more observers, and disputed interpretations are presented as comprehensively and fairly as possible.

Chapter 5 is concerned with lessons learned and with policy prescriptions, including options for the adaptation of U.S. policies in a changed security environment and an examination of whether there are clear parallels to other areas of security planning that may provide insights. A fundamental question is whether institutional arrangements and the resulting policy choices support long-term U.S. security objectives in a way that will allow the United States to maintain its position of leadership in a changing world order.

CHAPTER TWO

The Role of Nuclear Weapons
during the Cold War

NUCLEAR WEAPONS AND NUCLEAR STRATEGY have had a profound influence on U.S. conceptions of power, on the choice and character of alliances, on regional politics, and on the way in which domestic scientific, technical, bureaucratic, and military resources have been organized on their behalf. Five decades of reliance on nuclear weapons generated a vast domestic industry of theories, doctrines, and practical procedures to demonstrate how nuclear capabilities protect U.S. security. Those decades also gave rise to a complex planning apparatus responsible for ensuring a high state of readiness for nuclear weapons in the event deterrence fails. Often neglected by security specialists, plans for nuclear operations have played a determining role in influencing the structure and character of nuclear forces. This chapter discusses the policies that guided nuclear operations during the cold war and sets the stage for the discussion of the evolution of the role and missions of nuclear forces since the end of the cold war.

Deterrence Defined

For all of the technical complexity and emphasis on precision in planning nuclear operations, the United States progressively invested in the development and deployment of new weapons in support of an objective that was never strictly quantifiable—to deter aggression by holding at risk what an adversary "values most." In principle, defining what is valued by an adversary involves not only judgments about military capabilities but also some understanding of leaders' political, economic, and even cultural motivations. Leon Sloss, an architect of nuclear policy in the 1980s, summarizes it: "Because we have never really been certain what the enemy values and because we had lots of weapons . . . we have held at risk practically everything. This is how we have gotten to these targeting plans that I believe are excessive."[1]

Operationally, however, deterrence came to be defined predominantly (although not exclusively) as the ability to threaten an enemy's ability to wage nuclear war, a mission that justified ever growing requirements for more diverse, accurate, and dispersed nuclear weapons operating on high alert. The essential objective of deterring Soviet aggression has been subject to repeated efforts to define quantitatively. Estimates range from guidelines in the early 1960s that the United States needed to destroy 70–90 percent of Soviet targets, to criteria developed by Secretary of Defense Robert McNamara during the Kennedy administration requiring that the United States be able to destroy 25 percent of the Soviet population and 50 percent of its "war-waging" industrial capacity, to a requirement defined in the late 1980s for 1,500 so-called prompt, hard-target kill missile warheads needed to counter Soviet advances in multiple, independently targetable, land-based missiles. Current assessments suggest that the 70–90 percent targeting criterion remains a principal guideline. These publicly revealed data, however, do not begin to capture the full scope of the complex calculations that inform actual targeting plans, which are highly classified.[2]

Target categories included nuclear forces, command and control facilities, conventional forces, Soviet leadership, and war-supporting industries (a wide variety of infrastructure, including manufacturing firms, petroleum facilities, and power plants). A centralized plan, the single integrated operation plan (SIOP), established the procedures for the rapid deployment of anywhere from several hundred to tens of thousands of weapons as a way to deter Soviet attack and, in the event of the failure of deterrence, to limit damage to the United States by destroying Soviet nuclear forces before they could be launched. (Until the 1980s, the SIOP also contained target sets in China.) Force modernization and improvements in intelligence and computing capabilities were pursued to support the goal of achieving maximum damage expectancy and precise coverage against a growing and more diversified set of targets. The target base for allocating forces against the Soviet Union grew exponentially, to an estimated level of 16,000 individual targets by 1986.[3]

The initial impetus in 1960 for centralizing attack plans under the Strategic Air Command (SAC) in Omaha was to ensure the coordination of the three legs of the strategic triad. The targeting staff moved to a SAC base in Omaha not in the interest of isolation but, it was explained at the time, because that base had the only computer large enough to carry out highly complex calculations. Curtis Lemay remarks, "It was a hurry-up thing . . . my first reaction was this is a helluva place to be going because there wasn't anything out there except an Indian fighting post. I wondered how it came about. . . . I think it was to a large extent political."[4] Before this arrangement, nuclear plans developed by the Joint Chiefs of Staff (JCS) and the individual commands had created conflicting and duplicative guidelines for launching weapons, a system in which individual commanders "were inclined to emphasize the needs of their own commands over the objective of attack synchronization."[5]

The need for the massive and comprehensive destruction of Soviet targets, according to General Russell E. Dougherty, a former commander of SAC, was an obvious imperative of military planning. Why this is not widely understood, he argues, has to do with the distinct preoccupations of policymakers compared to those of military planners: "National leaders and policy-makers constantly grapple with abstractions and conceptual schisms presented by nuclear weapons: the debates on secondary nuclear effects, the search for the real anatomy of deterrence . . . and the disputes concerning the morality of nuclear war. By contrast, note the very real circumstances faced by the commander of a nuclear command. He cannot afford abstractions." Dougherty emphasizes the precision and reliability of nuclear operations. The "exacting nuclear planning done by the JSTPS [Joint Strategic Target Planning Staff], both in target selection and in preplanned application of weapons," which, along with the discipline and cohesion demanded of officers, supports the central objective of nuclear plans. Simply stated, the objective is victory: "The operational commander must win."[6]

The definition of what was sufficient to achieve a credible deterrent shifted over time in response to Soviet force improvements, to accommodate increases in U.S. forces, and as a result of advances in intelligence and in techniques for the construction of targeting plans. The science of targeting is highly demanding but not exact. In the past, the growth in the target list and higher demands for coverage of those targets typically corresponded with the growth in the stockpile of weapons. As a former deputy director of the joint strategic targeting and planning staff alleges regarding the plans of the 1980s, "The 10,000-plus [target base] is the result of accretion of the stockpile. We didn't get to where we are by a rational targeting policy, but through the number of weapons we had."[7]

Nuclear Weapons in the Cold War

Since the detonation of atomic bombs over Hiroshima and Nagasaki during World War II, U.S. nuclear strategy has relied on the logic that credible deterrence requires active preparation for the use of nuclear weapons, both to enhance deterrence and in the event that deterrence fails. As Dougherty summarizes it: "The better the [nuclear] command can strike against the full range of all threat targets, using as few as possible of the nuclear weapons of the command, the better U.S. chances are to deter any major conflict. The better the command, the less likely it will have to fight."[8] When the United States had a monopoly on atomic weapons, the air force defined the requirements of deterrence based on plans for the destruction of seventy Soviet cities using 133 low-yield bombs.[9] The threat to use massive air strikes in support of a strategy for "killing a nation," as General Curtis Lemay, former commander of U.S. Air Forces in Europe, describes it, was believed sufficient to deter any rational leader from initiating hostilities against the United States.

The first Soviet atomic test in August 1949, which caught the United States by surprise, altered the calculus of nuclear deterrence. Having seriously underestimated Soviet technical capabilities, U.S. policymakers and military planners set about to develop nuclear forces (beginning with the hydrogen bomb) and corresponding operational plans designed to counter any conceivable numerical or technical advantages sought by the enemy. By the mid-1950s, the Eisenhower administration replaced a small force capable of destroying cities with the requirement to match or exceed the capabilities of adversaries, maintaining sufficient weapons, a high state of preparedness, and a steady pace of innovation to

21

hedge against technological surprises or the potential failure of any element of the U.S. force structure.

The threat of sudden technological "breakout" by the adversary and the intent of Soviet leaders to engage in concerted aggression and surprise attack have informed nuclear force planning for more than four decades. A corollary belief is an enduring sense of U.S. vulnerability and relative inferiority, reflected in controversies over the "bomber gap" and the "missile gap" of the 1950s and 1960s or threats of a disarming attack on U.S. land-based missiles, known as the "window of vulnerability" in the late 1970s and early 1980s. The belief that the United States was chronically behind the Soviet Union was the impetus behind countless modernization programs and force improvements. As Lyndon B. Johnson, then a U.S. senator, stated after the Soviets launched the Sputnik satellite in 1957, "Our country is disturbed over the tremendous military and scientific achievement of Russia. . . . It would appear that we have slipped dangerously behind."[10]

Uncertainty about the other side's intentions, exacerbated by limited intelligence even about the size of the Soviet arsenal, impelled worst-case planning. Beginning in 1955, the threat of a Soviet surprise attack, motivated by either a perceived imbalance in U.S. forces or any sign of weakness in U.S. resolve, became the most demanding scenario against which the U.S. military had to prepare. The potentially paralyzing effects of a surprise attack on the ability of the United States to retaliate encouraged the diversification and expansion of the nuclear arsenal. This buildup began with a massive increase in the production of weapons in the 1950s and 1960s and the development of new kinds of delivery systems, including long-range ballistic missiles and advanced naval platforms, such as submarines.

The steady growth of nuclear arsenals was not impelled by empirical calculations of the size or character of opposing forces or the optimal number of weapons needed to arm delivery systems. The buildup of the U.S. nuclear weapons stockpile in the 1950s reflected the greater efficiency of weapons production facilities, rising to 30,000 warheads by the early 1960s. The Soviet Union, similarly, produced 45,000 nuclear weapons by the mid-1980s, well in excess of what could be used even in an all-out war. The United States has long relied on a triad of long-range bombers, intercontinental ballistic missiles, and submarine-launched ballistic missiles (SLBM) kept in a state of high readiness and targeted mainly on forces and military installations spread across what was then the vast territory of the USSR. The rationale for a triad of nuclear capabilities had at least as much to do with competition among the services for nuclear missions as with any articulated military imperative.[11]

To fulfill its security commitments to NATO, the United States planned to initiate the use of nuclear weapons to deter conventional aggression through the Warsaw Pact, escalating to central strategic confrontation if necessary, in furtherance of the long-standing policy of flexible response. Until 1991, the United States maintained ground-based and sea-based tactical nuclear weapons deployed overseas to defend against Soviet and Warsaw Pact aggression, along with air-based forces—a number of which remain stationed in Europe.[12] U.S. nuclear security assurances to other allies such as Japan and South Korea, in turn, served the dual purposes of extending deterrence and of dissuading such states from acquiring their own nuclear arsenals.

The creation of a survivable Soviet nuclear force beginning in the 1960s, along with the growth of quantitatively superior conventional forces in the Warsaw Pact, imposed demands on the United States to develop new ways to deter and target hostile forces. In addition to deploying large numbers of tactical nuclear weapons in Europe and Asia and on naval vessels (and developing selective and limited options for their use), strategic forces of greater accuracy and lethality were deployed against a growing array of Soviet nuclear (and other military) targets, resulting in an arsenal in excess of 10,000 deployed weapons by the mid-1980s.[13]

A strategy of massive retaliation in the 1950s and 1960s—launching the bulk of the U.S. arsenal in a single, massive operation—gave way to new concepts of limited nuclear options and the need for "invulnerable second-strike forces" capable of destroying the Soviet Union after it had attacked first. In the effort to dampen the instabilities and costs of the nuclear rivalry, arms control negotiations beginning in the late 1960s established ceilings on deployments as a way to ensure that each side could retain survivable retaliatory forces. The codification of a rough parity of survivable forces accorded some measure of predictability, even as both sides continued to modernize and enhance their respective capabilities to hold the other at risk. Ensuring the survivability of forces against a surprise attack, however, lent impetus to continuous force innovations, including submarines with stealth capabilities, hardened underground silos for land-based missiles, protracted consideration of mobile deployment schemes, and high-alert levels for the bomber force (ceased by the Bush administration in 1991) and ballistic missiles.

Arms control negotiations until the late 1980s sought agreements to establish numerical ceilings on deployed forces, not the elimination of weapon systems. Although there is a large body of literature about what constituted strategic parity, or calculations to determine crisis stability, strategic sufficiency, and other ways to quantify a strategic balance, the foundations for stability were chronically in conflict with competitive force modernization programs. Disparities in the character of the two sides' force postures, with the Soviets relying on multiple-warhead, land-based missiles for almost two-thirds of their deterrent force and the United States relying on them for less than one-third, made it technically and politically difficult to agree on what constituted equitable limits. Despite U.S. superiority in bombers and sea-based systems, there were protracted debates in the 1970s and 1980s about how Soviet superiority in land-based forces created a disproportionate level of U.S. vulnerability, which had to be redressed to avoid preemptive attack or political blackmail.

Since the 1960s, nuclear planners have been preoccupied with the vulnerability of the U.S. nuclear command system to even small preemptive attacks. A study prepared by the Institute for Defense Analysis in 1975, for example, quotes an assessment from 1960 that the response time for a president to react to a tactical warning of an attack before impact "is between *zero and about 15 minutes. In using the upper extreme of 15 minutes,* he will be assuming that every procedural and physical element in the whole warning and strategic command and control structure works perfectly and that the enemy will not employ SLBMs or sabotage effectively against it," a level of performance that was considered unlikely.[14] The improvements in strategic weapons in the 1970s and 1980s allowing for greater speed, precision, and lethality of deployed weapons increasingly imposed demands on command arrangements that would allow for the prompt launch of potentially vulnerable systems at the first sign of attack.[15] Rapid reaction characterized both the U.S. and the Soviet command systems. The premium put on options for the prompt use of forces in the event of crisis was an effort to resolve the fundamental constraint imposed by the vulnerabilities of communications, command, and control systems to survive even a relatively small, surprise attack.

For policymakers, deciding when the United States would employ its forces against a nuclear attack—launching on warning, after certain detonation, or only after riding out a full-scale nuclear strike—remains controversial. The debates about launch doctrines have focused largely on whether a policy to ride out an attack would degrade the ability of the United States to respond and thus perhaps make war more likely by undercutting deterrence; or conversely, whether a policy of launch on warning would impose undue pressure on U.S. and Russian national command authorities, which could lead to catastrophic misjudgment. Keeping forces on high alert and other operational procedures sustained during the cold war implies a readiness to launch promptly, official reluctance to define policy formally notwithstanding.[16]

The determination of requisite target coverage and alert levels to uphold strategy has long resided with the nuclear command. Military responsibility for planning the details of military operations has not been in question. "Development of the SIOP is a purely military function," a former Pentagon official says.[17] Guidance for the implementation of strategy (known as policy guidance for the employment of nuclear weapons, or NUWEP) is provided by political authorities to give direction to the Joint Chiefs in developing the assessment of threats and corresponding operational plans—the joint strategic planning document (JSPD) and the joint strategic capabilities plans (JSCP). The ultimate authority for civilian guidance resides with the president. It is the responsibility of the nuclear commands to then translate these directives—described by a former Pentagon official as a "broad blueprint . . . used to provide a statement of approved strategy"—into detailed preparations for nuclear employment.[18] Plans have been altered periodically to accommodate technological and political changes or differing perceptions of the importance of particular nuclear missions in successive administrations—from the need to conduct limited nuclear operations under the policy of flexible response beginning in the 1960s, to the ability to prevail in a nuclear war articulated in the 1970s, to a more robust commitment to war waging and the potential for protracted nuclear engagement advanced in the 1980s.

Until 1991, the commander in chief of the Strategic Air Command served as the principal officer in charge of managing the joint strategic target planning staff (JSTPS), a staff of about 300 military officers from each of the services. (The JSTPS has since been replaced by staff operating under the J-5, or policy and plans, division of the Joint Chiefs of Staff.) The JSTPS was established in 1960 to develop integrated operational plans, including the coordination of strategic forces and nuclear forces assigned to CINCLANT and CINCPAC. Operating at SAC headquarters in Omaha, the JSTPS maintained two separate directorates, one to prepare a strategic target list and the other to assign weapons to targets in the SIOP, in accordance with specified priorities and damage expectancies. The overall guidance for these plans flowed from the direction prepared by the Office of the Secretary of Defense (OSD) and translated by the Joint Chiefs of Staff into the joint strategic capabilities plan (JSCP). In addition, the chiefs prepared the joint strategic planning document (JSPD), which served as the basis for policy discussion with the president and the National Security Council about military strategy and force requirements. The official defense guidance, finally, articulated the general principles of military strategy approved by senior political authorities, including the president. The structure of this command has changed since 1992, although it retains many of the same functions, discussed further below.

There are highly routinized procedures, in short, through which political authorities indicate their intentions to military planners and through which targeting officials seek approval for needed changes. Indeed, the system is set up for ample checks and balances and allows for a reasonable division of labor. As the commander in chief, the president retains the formal authority for determining national strategy. More detailed guidance flows from the secretary of defense, who, by law, occupies a place in the chain of command between the president and the military commanders. As Latham described the system in the late 1980s, "Revisions to the SIOP . . . result in periodic briefings on the changes to the secretary [of defense] and his staff. These processes provide assurance, through civilian oversight, that the final military operational plans conform to national objectives, strategy and policy."[19]

Political Authority

Innovations in operational plans sought by political authorities have been met with skepticism by military planners on numerous occasions. For most of the cold war, there was active tension between political efforts to devise options for limited nuclear strikes and the preference of planners for centralized plans and rapid execution of strategic forces before an enemy strike could disrupt the command system or destroy U.S. forces. According to a former air force chief of staff, "Flexible response was useful to build up the edifice and give structure to a myth."[20] Directives calling for more flexible operations had been issued for years but did not begin to affect planning significantly until 1980. Henry Rowen summarized this tension in 1975: "From an operator's viewpoint, a nuclear exchange in which the politicians try to mastermind the conflict while keeping the commanders from carrying out what they regard as necessary military operations could be a frightening prospect."[21] General Dougherty affirms this perspective: "U.S. military commands are conditioned for prompt responses to crisp, unequivocal military orders to pursue well-defined actions. . . . Execution orders for nuclear strikes that are spawned in protracted and acrimonious debate at the NCA level, schisms with congressional leaders, and vitriolic internal cabinet debate are sure to stretch military discipline to the limit."[22] In another instance, there was a high degree of skepticism among planners about directives issued by the Reagan administration to assure "continuity in government" as part of a strategy of protracted war, a policy that many military planners thought diverted critical resources for objectives that were not compelling.[23]

The determination of the precise level and character of forces needed to uphold strategy, as mentioned above, has rarely been a preoccupation of elected and appointed officials. Few presidents or White House aides have spent time on operational issues, apart from routine but infrequent SIOP briefings, and sustained attention by senior officials in the Office of the Secretary of Defense is, with a few notable exceptions, rare. One military official who had responsibility for preparing the JSCP claimed in 1988 that civilians were "criminally negligent" when it came to oversight, leaving the details to the joint staff or the JSTPS. "We would just cut deals as junior officers [of the different services] in allocating weapons," he explained. "Sometimes this resulted in remarkable changes in the guidance, which should have been reviewed at the highest level."[24] For the most part, revisions involved expansions of the target list not for reasons of policy but to accommodate or request new weapons.

According to participants at the time, Frank Miller, who served as the director of strategic forces policy in the Office of the Secretary of Defense in the 1980s, was the first civilian to successfully delve into core details of the SIOP, for which access was by no means granted automatically. Working with a military assistant who was knowledgeable about the JSTPS, Miller got access to the documents that described the revisions to the SIOP that had been implemented by staff but not cleared by OSD or the Joint Chiefs—so-called revision reports. A military officer who was part of this effort calls Miller's access "historic. . . . It happened just because of the serendipity of some young guy who knew where the skeletons were buried."[25]

Briefings to senior officials about the SIOP typically were perfunctory and, often, unintelligible. The thousands of pages of SIOP data and computer codes contained in the plans would be translated into an hour-long briefing and presented in several dozen view graphs. "Generally, no one at the briefings wanted to ask questions because they didn't want to embarrass themselves," according to one account, in reference to both military and political authorities.[26] Whether strategy perceived at the political level has ever been in conformity with the underlying plans is debatable, although some reforms in oversight and the direction of planning priorities have since been implemented.

The Bush Legacy

Even before the sweeping political changes culminating in the fall of the Berlin Wall in 1989, civilian officials in the Pentagon had begun to more closely examine nuclear targeting plans and operational objectives. A major restructuring of the SIOP was undertaken in 1988, for example, as part of an ongoing effort to implement more flexible targeting capabilities, to reevaluate targeting criteria, and to reduce the time needed to construct plans in order to be more responsive to changes in policies, threats, and force innovations. At the time, Major General Richard Goetze, deputy chief of staff for strategic planning at SAC, proclaimed, "The bottom line is that we can expect today's rigid preplanned SIOP, requiring months to build and change, to be a thing of the past."[27] A new SIOP was implemented in 1991, although it was soon outstripped by the momentous changes in the Soviet Union.

The need to adapt nuclear policies to reflect the changing realities in the Soviet Union were readily apparent to President George Bush and his key advisers early in his administration. The fragility of political conditions in the fragmenting Soviet bloc—including pervasive and

profound economic dislocation in Russia and other republics and growing pressure on the Russian government to provide alternative means
of occupation for salient sectors of the Russian economy, not least members of the Russian military elite—called for bold U.S. initiatives to help
counter potential instability. The primary concern was to ensure effective and enduring controls over the Soviet nuclear arsenal, including
an estimated 27,000 tactical and strategic weapons dispersed across
Soviet territory. Ensuring the safety of nuclear weapons against compromise, centralizing authority and security for the nuclear assets of
the former Soviet republics in Russia, and preventing the dissemination or use of nuclear technologies and expertise among new nations
became the most pressing objectives of nuclear diplomacy during Bush's
term.[28]

Of the Soviet total, an estimated 15,000 tactical weapons were deployed outside of Russia, across a majority of Soviet republics. Following the August 1991 Moscow coup and the creation of the Common-
wealth of Independent States, the Bush administration moved quickly
to devise measures to consolidate control over, and to secure, the Soviet
nuclear arsenal. This included a series of unilateral measures to prompt
reciprocal actions by the Russian government, including the elimination of all ground-based tactical missile warheads, removal of tactical
weapons from naval vessels, the de-alerting of bombers (as well as missiles slated for cancellation by START), and cancellation of U.S. land-
based missile programs (including the M-X, the mobile single-warhead
Midgetman missile, and a short-range system known as S-RAM).

Secretary of Defense Richard Cheney, along with General Colin L.
Powell, chairman of the Joint Chiefs of Staff , also recognized early on
that many of the premises and a large percentage of the targets in the
SIOP were being rendered obsolete, as a result of both reductions in
forces under START and abrupt changes in the Soviet bloc. Cheney began in 1989 to ask questions about the SIOP as part of his consideration
of proposals for force reductions being advanced by the Soviets. He
soon realized that his principal aides were not informed about such
details, however. Cheney issued a directive in November 1989 calling
for a full-scale review of the SIOP, to be chaired by General Robert Herres,
vice chairman of the Joint Chiefs. After eighteen months, the study was
concluded and briefings were prepared for the secretary and the chairman of the Joint Chiefs. From the outset, Cheney and Powell were reportedly appalled by the presentations put before them.[29] The details

revealed about operational plans persuaded them that the SIOP was not only out of date but also devoid of clear objectives or apparent logic. According to one account, "Cheney concluded the SIOP was not a nuclear war plan . . . it seemed just like a jumble of processed data. . . . Every time the Pentagon had bought a new nuclear weapons system to match the Soviet's. . .Omaha had simply found targets for the added warheads and rearranged the SIOP math formulas. This had gone on for years, as captains and majors who wrote the SIOP rotated in and out."[30]

Despite the heroic efforts to develop systems and software needed to devise and coordinate precise plans, officers charged with covering different target sets developed models to target multiple weapons on the same target, with no apparent knowledge of what other programmers were doing. Some industrial centers in Moscow, for example, had multiple weapons allocated to specified, individual factories despite the fact that the buildings were closely clustered. The ten warhead M-X missiles, with a target coverage of more than three miles, were targeted on areas less than a mile apart. And nearly forty weapons were designated just to hit Kiev. In one of the SIOP briefings prepared for Cheney, a video demonstrated "weapons lay-down" techniques, using small red dots added incrementally to demonstrate the pattern of warheads targeted on a particular site in the Soviet Union. According to the recollection of one participant, "Moscow turned slowly into a solid red, covered over and over with ludicrous targets. Cheney started squirming around and finally asked one of his military aides why we were doing this kind of thing. 'Ask Mr. Nuke,' the aide responded sarcastically," referring to Frank Miller, the principal civilian architect of the joint strategic capabilities plan.[31]

After years of effort by Miller and others to devise limited options that a president could use to control escalation, what was described as a limited attack option in the SIOP included "withhold" options, which avoided targets in Moscow but directed warheads against its suburbs. Strikes against sites other than forces or command centers, such as industrial and transportation infrastructure, were planned without reference to their proximity to where Soviet leadership or nuclear forces were located. The standard and accepted assumptions of damage expectancy, moreover, took into account only the immediate effects of a nuclear strike, not secondary effects such as fire, fallout, and persistent contamination. Some degree of redundant targeting, especially against high-priority and hardened targets such as missile silos, was accepted and never challenged by officials. Conservative estimates of lethality also were believed to be appropriate in light of the uncertain (and disputed) significance of secondary effects. But damage expectancies and other quantitative criteria to be used to help set priorities among targets had "evolved into a set of requirements."[32]

What Cheney's review uncovered amounted to a fundamental breakdown in the coherence of political and operational policies. The dilemma of conflicting plans generated by the services before 1960 not only eluded resolution but seemed to have been compounded by modern computing, specialization, and remoteness from the world of policy. The planning problems did not occur because of misguided commitment to warfighting at SAC. The "dedication to precision and reliability," which Dougherty hailed as the hallmark of JSTPS in 1987, instead foundered in the crippling complexities and vague guidance that have been the hallmarks of planning for many years.[33] The innovations undertaken by Bush officials involved the elimination of thousands of targets from the SIOP. Former Soviet republics were removed entirely, many leadership targets were reduced to reflect the collapse of communism, and the need to attack tactical nuclear installations or transportation links outside of Russia was deemed no longer necessary after weapons were consolidated on Russian territory. Many industrial and war-supporting target options were eliminated. In 1991, SAC was abolished in favor of a single unified command, renamed STRATCOM. Some consideration at very senior levels was given to more dramatic reconfigurations of the nuclear posture, such as a dyad of bombers and submarines, but these were not pursued to conclusion.[34]

After General Butler was appointed head of SAC in 1991, major initiatives to reinvent planning assumptions and procedures of planning were undertaken. In addition to the restructuring of the nuclear command, a strategic planning study group established by Butler in 1992 was directed to develop a new planning process for global application. Methods were developed for "adaptive targeting," allowing for rapid and flexible retargeting of "spontaneous threats which are more likely to emerge in a new international environment unconstrained by the Super Power stand-off."[35] These changes, based on "continuous analysis of guidance, forces, and target changes," led to the approval of a new SIOP in July 1993.[36]

Nuclear Weapons at the End of the Cold War

The successes of the Bush administration in reaching sweeping arms control agreements and other cooperative arrangements with Russia provided the newly elected president Bill Clinton with an ambitious agenda based on bipartisan support. The agenda was unprecedented in both the scope of its provisions and the potential for further stabilizing actions in the future. After twelve years of negotiations and three years after signature, START I entered into force on December 5, 1994, requiring the United States and Russia to reduce their respective nuclear forces to no more than 6,000 nuclear warheads, a cut of almost half of deployed weapons for each side. The agreement set an ambitious schedule for required dismantlement of launchers under intrusive verification and accounting procedures. It also required three former Soviet republics (Belarus, Kazakhstan, and Ukraine) to eliminate nuclear weapons on their territory and to accede unconditionally to the Nuclear Non-Proliferation Treaty (NPT) as nuclear weapons–free states, a process completed in late 1994. (Both sides began active dismantlement programs before START I's formal entry into force, however.)

START II, which was signed in early 1993 and ratified by the United States in 1996, further requires the United States and Russia to reduce the number of deployed strategic warheads to a level not to exceed 3,500 on each side and would eliminate all heavy and multiple-warhead intercontinental ballistic missiles, the most destabilizing element of the two sides force postures (see table 2-1). In an effort to reduce Russian opposition to START II, which hinges in part on the financial burdens imposed on Russia as a result of the costs of required dismantlement and the need to deploy a new single-warhead missile to restore Russia's numerical parity under START II limits, the United States in early 1997 proposed START III, which would relax the timetable for Russian reductions and, contingent on START II ratification, negotiate a new warhead level of 2,000–2,500. As of this writing, the Russian Duma has yet to ratify the treaty, but the Joint Chiefs have given their approval for a level of 2,000–2,500 deployed weapons under START III. This is for now the specified threshold below which U.S. planners assert they could no longer fulfill the demands of nuclear deterrence. A senior STRATCOM official asserted in mid-1997, "It is not clear that the United States could be a superpower and maintain its security commitments with fewer that 2,500 weapons."[37]

Table 2-1. Nuclear Arsenals, Russia and the United States, START I, START II, START III

Country	Before START	START I (July 31, 1991)	Current suspected strategic nuclear weapons	Current suspected nonstrategic nuclear weapons	Total suspected nuclear weapons	START II, Phase I (January 3, 1993)	START II, Phase II (strategic total in 2003)	START III
Russia	10,780	10,682	7,200	6,000–13,000	13,200–20,200	3,800–4,250	3,100	2,000–2,500
United States	12,720	11,080	8,500	7,000	15,500	3,800–4,250	3,500	2,000–2,500
Total	23,500	21,762	~15,700	~13,000–20,000	~18,700–35,700	~7,600–8,500	6,600	4,000–5,000

Source: Center for Defense Information's Nuclear Weapons Database; U.S. Arms Control and Disarmament Agency's Facts and Figures; and Federation of American Scientists' Nuclear Resources.

The Bush nuclear legacy, moreover, was not confined to reductions in the level of strategic forces. Included were important steps to reassure Russia, including measures to de-alert land-based Minuteman II missiles (reconfiguring safety switches to prevent ignition of the motors) and separating bombers from their nuclear payload.[38] The administration also supported continued adherence to the Anti-Ballistic Missile Treaty, subject to negotiations to allow for the development of theater missile defenses, and pledged support for a comprehensive test ban. The Comprehensive Test Ban Treaty was endorsed formally by the United States at the NPT review conference in 1995 and adopted and opened for signature in September 1996. While reaffirming the importance of the Anti-Ballistic Missile Treaty, the Clinton administration also has pursued extensive negotiations with Russia to discuss the demarcation between theater ballistic missile defenses and anti-ballistic missile systems, to allow for the development and deployment of the former in compliance with the treaty's limits on national defense systems. The issue of what is and is not consistent with the treaty—and whether the agreement is still in the security interests of the United States—has become a major element of contention between the executive branch, the Congress, and outside supporters or critics of defenses, a political struggle that has had a defining influence on the administration's negotiating position and future defense modernization plans.[39]

The challenge of nuclear weapons was transformed in a few short years from a declared need to prevail in a strategic nuclear conflict, should deterrence fail, to a new set of concerns stemming from the requirement to establish fail-safe controls on the remainder of the global nuclear arsenal: among these controls were building a cooperative relationship with Russia in furtherance of additional reductions in nuclear forces and preventing new states from acquiring or threatening to use nuclear weapons. The change in mission was captured in September 1992 by General George Lee Butler, commander of the Strategic Command, when he announced that the United States in 1989 had "abandoned the concept of global war with the Soviet Union as the principal planning and programming paradigm for the U.S. armed forces."[40] As for deterrence, it was widely argued that the United States could respond to any conceivable remaining nuclear threat with a fraction of its cold war nuclear arsenal. It was against this backdrop that the Clinton administration undertook a formal review of the nuclear force posture and considered the utility and potential missions of nuclear weapons against new adversaries.

CHAPTER THREE

The 1993–94
Nuclear Posture Review

THE CLINTON ADMINISTRATION entered office in 1993 with a mandate for change, a term used repeatedly by the candidate Clinton and understood to mean sweeping reforms, albeit with a clear emphasis on domestic issues. Clinton's victory at the polls was widely interpreted as the result of his commitment to a new social agenda and the public's apparent disaffection with the economic status quo. His vision for foreign policy, to say nothing of his national security policy, was not widely understood or, for many voters, considered particularly important. President Clinton nevertheless inherited a challenging and highly activist security agenda from his predecessor: major nuclear force reduction agreements still to be implemented and a series of innovative cooperative ventures with Russia and the former Soviet republics to advance the common objectives of denuclearization and threat reduction.[1]

The rapid pace of external change and the momentum behind the Bush initiatives suggested to many that a transformation of U.S. nuclear policy was well under way. The overarching threat of a concerted attack from Russian strategic rocket forces had diminished. The agreement reached in January 1994 to detarget missiles from each sides' territories, though symbolic, was seen as a vital step in building mutual confidence.[2] As the Russians moved to comply with the dismantling of weapons mandated by START, the nuclear establishment of the former Soviet Union declined precipitously both in its capabilities to wage war and in the reliability of its command and control system. As a result, the focus of nuclear dangers shifted to the potential disintegration of authority over the weapons and technologies left in the wake of the cold war. White House statements increasingly emphasized the cordiality between the United States and Russia in the early 1990s and, in furtherance of a deeper partnership, the need for "concrete steps to adapt the nuclear forces and practices on both sides to the changed international security situation."[3]

The elaborate targeting plans in the single integrated operation plan (SIOP), which included Russian conventional forces and economic assets, also were believed to be out of sync with the realities of a state whose economy and armed forces were close to collapse. "The dispirited and disaffected Russian military may be a greater danger to its own government," one analyst notes, "than to any foreign state."[4] Even without Russian ratification of START II, Russia's nuclear arsenal had diminished significantly, along with its command and control systems. The numbers of weapons thought essential to provide requisite target coverage in the early 1990s, even after the Cheney reforms, were widely thought to be well in excess of any conceivable nuclear contingency. As for regional aggressors, a small portion of the U.S. nuclear arsenal seemed sufficient to deter, retaliate, or even threaten preemptive attack against any emerging nuclear powers if necessary. As the same military analyst summarizes it, "It seems unlikely that a state with a handful of nuclear weapons would view the U.S. nuclear deterrent differently at 3,500 warheads instead of 7,000 or 1,500 instead of 3,500."[5]

With the changing character of Russian and global nuclear dangers, policies guiding U.S. nuclear forces, arms control, and nonproliferation became more directly linked. Efforts to remove nuclear weapons from the territories of three former Soviet republics—Ukraine, Kazakhstan, and Belarus—required that these countries be persuaded of the benefits of supporting the Nuclear Non-Proliferation Treaty (NPT) and other nonproliferation arrangements, including the Lisbon Protocol, which confirmed the agreement to remove nuclear weapons from the three former Soviet republics. Political disaffection among members of the NPT, scheduled for a final review and a vote on its extension in April 1995, held out the possibility that the centerpiece of nonproliferation could unravel and with it the fledgling agreements to denuclearize the former Soviet republics. For states in the former Soviet Union, in particular, it was vitally important to promote a concept of security in which nuclear weapons could be seen as an outright political and military liability.[6] Holding the international regime together in the 1995 review conference required the administration to demonstrate that the United States and other nuclear powers had made progress toward nuclear disarmament, including a comprehensive ban on nuclear testing, deeper reductions in their own arsenals, and a clear commitment by the United States to stand by its long-standing policy not to target nonnuclear countries unless they are allied in aggression with a nuclear power.[7]

The administration also faced severe fiscal challenges as it tried to harmonize the goals of reducing the defense budget and supporting missions vital to U.S. security interests. In the aftermath of Desert Storm, the primacy of superior conventional technologies and the so-called reconnaissance strike complex dominated conceptions of U.S. global military strategy. In a climate of austerity, the costs of maintaining strategic forces competed directly with new requirements for conventional capabilities. The professional military, especially the army and the navy and with the notable exception of the submarine community, seemed increasingly disinterested in nuclear weapons, in any case, especially when it came to triage decisions over resources.

There continues to be increasing support in elements of the military for an explicit strategy to deemphasize nuclear forces in favor of more vigorous investment in advanced conventional weapons, capturing the resources currently dedicated to nuclear missions. A recently issued report of a panel of military experts appointed by the Congress to comment on the Pentagon's Quadrennial Defense Review, for example, offered this conclusion: "Advancing military technologies that merge the capabilities of information systems with precision-guided weaponry and real-time targeting and other new weapon systems may provide a supplement or an alternative to the nuclear arsenals of the Cold War." The report also urged the administration to acknowledge the security benefits of moving to lower levels of forces called for under START III, with or without Russian ratification of START II.[8]

Even without the pressure of external change, shrinking resources, or a shift in political parties, it is the common impulse of every new administration to review the priorities of its predecessor. In the Clinton administration, the call was for fundamental reevaluation of the basic premises and objectives of all defense programs. Aptly named the Bottom-Up Review, the first initiative, beginning in the summer of 1993, focused on conventional forces. It was an attempt to rationalize and win consensus for a post–cold war strategy that would fulfill vital missions with drastically reduced resources. The Bottom-Up Review modest conclusions, borne of protracted clashes within the bureaucracy and a reluctance to antagonize congressional and other constituents of particular defense programs, presaged the challenges of the Nuclear Posture Review, which followed a few months later.

Insight into the likely direction of the new administration's nuclear policies first came with the appointment of Les Aspin, former chairman of the House Armed Services Committee, as Clinton's first secretary of defense. Along with several civilian defense experts in key subordinate positions, Aspin's new role suggested that the first post–cold war Pentagon was to be guided by individuals who helped pioneer programs to reduce nuclear dangers in the crumbling Soviet empire, convinced that nuclear security was increasingly a matter of cooperative efforts to prevent loss of control over nuclear weapons and materials. As a member of Congress, Les Aspin emphasized the urgency of cooperative measures, such as the program that came to be known as cooperative threat reduction. Also, before his appointment as secretary of defense, Aspin articulated doubts about the relevance of nuclear deterrence for redressing modern security threats. In addition to the dissolution of authority in Russia, Aspin stressed the rise of aggressive third world states seeking "weapons of mass destruction"—states whose ambitions were unlikely to be tamed by traditional superpower strategy. More pointedly, he argued that "a world without nuclear weapons would actually be better. Nuclear weapons are still the big equalizer, but the United States is not the equalizer but the equalizee."[9]

Was Aspin's perspective representative of the prevailing logic within the new administration? In truth, it was never clear where the administration was headed, largely because the president addressed nuclear issues so rarely. The administration's earliest statements nevertheless indicated a commitment to an ambitious arms control agenda, one that would require policy innovations if only to implement the many agreements and reforms undertaken by President Bush. The highly publicized call for a fundamental review of the role and purpose of nuclear weapons, moreover, led many to believe that this presaged ambitious efforts to expand upon the alterations in the U.S. nuclear posture initiated by the preceding administration. With both houses of Congress under Democratic control and the heightened stature accorded to new administrations, many who favored change thought this was a moment of maximum opportunity for the president to establish a nuclear legacy consonant with emerging security challenges.

The review of nuclear forces was postponed until after the Bottom-Up Review was completed, a reflection of the greater urgency given to budgetary imperatives, which conventional force requirements dominated. Aside from the political sensitivities involved in reviewing nuclear forces, the prevailing assumption among defense officials was that the cost savings from cuts in strategic forces were likely to be negligible. This common perception has been challenged internally by some budget analysts and in an unclassified analysis of the costs of maintaining nuclear forces and the nuclear infrastructure.[10] The formal conduct of the Nuclear Posture Review did not begin until the fall of 1993. The administration encountered both service and congressional criticism early on, however, for its failure to consider fully the interrelationships among conventional and nuclear requirements. Key decisions affecting future force structure, basing, and infrastructure (including, inter alia, the requirements for dual-capable bomber force levels) were raised in the Bottom-Up Review before the conclusion of the Nuclear Posture Review.[11]

The Nuclear Posture Review began as a White House–sanctioned Pentagon study, to be carried out under the direction of civilian officials in cooperation with military officers.[12] According to several participants, it was a microcosm of Aspin's zeal to systematically reorganize national security policy and to implement the ambitious structural reforms in the Pentagon that he—as a "defense intellectual" and a member of the moderate wing of the military reform movement—had long considered. As described by Aspin, the review was to be an exhaustive exercise in political-military analysis, an effort to match the design of forces with the political objectives that nuclear deterrence was meant to uphold. It would differ from other Pentagon initiatives in several respects, including its emphasis on the fundamentally political character of nuclear policy and the diminishing importance of strategic operations for deterring future threats. Requirements would derive from policy, looking to, as Aspin put it, "where . . . you go after START II."[13] The study would "incorporate reviews of policy, doctrine, force structure, operations, safety and security, and arms control in one look."[14]

Despite this broad mandate, involvement in or approval by other concerned agencies was apparently never considered seriously. While many assumed that the study would be subject to further review—"not a Defense Department fait accompli," as a senior official in the National

Security Council put it—Pentagon officials apparently never considered outside participation to be necessary or desirable.[15] "We certainly weren't about to invite any weirdos from ACDA [Arms Control and Disarmament Agency]," said one Pentagon participant. "It was the Aspin-Clinton show," he added, to be conducted in the freewheeling way Aspin was accustomed to and reinforced by the apparent confidence of the president in Aspin's leadership and intellect.[16] The terms of reference for the review, drafted from guidance given by Secretary Aspin, called for an outside panel of experts to critique the process as it evolved. But despite the obvious importance accorded to political considerations and a growing interdependency among U.S. nuclear force plans, U.S.-Russian diplomacy, and nonproliferation policy, no interagency or outside review ever occurred.

Even for those familiar with the difficulties commonly encountered in efforts to win support of the defense bureaucracy for initiatives that appear to impinge on long-standing programs or objectives, there were reasons to believe that the nuclear posture review could produce results, at least as long as Aspin was at the helm. The review was portrayed as a genuine effort to create a nuclear tabula rasa from which creative thinking and ambitious reform proposals would emerge. Why not? The mandate was wide open and had the backing of the secretary of defense and the support of the president. Seemingly like-minded individuals were in charge, and, as many thought at the time, there were no obvious or compelling substantive reasons for opposition.

The resignation of Les Aspin in January 1994 gave leadership responsibility for the review to John Deutch, who replaced William Perry, the deputy secretary of defense, after Perry was appointed to succeed Aspin. As quickly became evident, this shift left the review without a senior-level champion. In addition to Deutch, joint stewardship for the effort had already been delegated to Admiral William Owens, vice chairman of the Joint Chiefs of Staff, who was assisted by Admiral Henry Chiles, commander in chief of the Strategic Forces Command (STRATCOM). Operational responsibility was shared by Ashton Carter, assistant secretary of defense for nuclear security and counterproliferation (later renamed assistant secretary of defense for international security policy), and Lieutenant General Barry McCaffrey, who was shortly thereafter replaced by Lieutenant General Wesley Clark. To carry out the directives and conduct analysis, working groups were established, each to examine specific aspects of the role of nuclear weapons in U.S. security, from force structure to deterrence strategy to plans and operations (see figure 3-1).[17]

According to numerous participants and observers, the initial enthusiasm of Ashton Carter, who was closely allied with both Secretary Aspin and his successor, William Perry, suggested a sincere belief in the power of analysis to change thinking and overthrow orthodoxy. As one report described the process: "[Ashton Carter] appointed six working groups staffed by uniformed officers and civilians to hold closed-door hearings at the Pentagon. . . . He urged them to free themselves from Cold War thinking and consider the issues creatively. . . . Everything was up for grabs."[18] His statements to colleagues at the time emphasized his determination to implement changes in the nuclear establishment in a way that would fundamentally transform its cold war preoccupations and force a recognition of the inherent risks in the existing nuclear posture.

Even the media picked up on Carter's enthusiasm. Articles in the *Washington Post* in March and April 1995 by David B. Ottaway and Steve Coll heralded Carter's commitment to and leadership of an ambitious review that was going to reinvent nuclear strategy. The journalists referred to Carter as a "minor cult figure in Washington's small but intense community of nuclear weapons specialists," especially, they stressed, "those who favored rapid reduction or elimination of nuclear weapons." They also emphasized that Carter was "interested especially in the hair-trigger alert status and 24-hour operations required of nuclear forces by the SIOP" and in seeking the elimination of those elements of the posture that most contributed to this situation, such as land-based missiles. They cited an article Carter wrote before his Pentagon appointment in which he stressed the opportunity for the United States and Russia to achieve "freedom from dependence on alerting and warning and, above all, freedom from reliance on prompt response."[19] Carter has since discounted this characterization of his views while he was in office and dismisses the significance of the nuclear posture review except as a force-planning exercise to guide the implementation of START II. Several of his colleagues in the Pentagon, however, assert that these and similar accounts of the review reflect Carter's objectives accurately and that Carter granted media interviews fairly freely.[20]

From its inception, the rhetoric of the review as articulated by Aspin and Carter struck some Pentagon professionals as implying a zealous assault on the accepted procedures and lines of authority that had long

Figure 3-1. *Structure of the Nuclear Posture Review*

```
                  ┌──────────────────────────┐
                  │   U.S. security strategy │
                  └────────────┬─────────────┘
                               ↓
                  ┌──────────────────────────┐
            ┌────→│      Role of nuclear     │←────┐
            │     │  weapons in U.S. security│     │
            │     └────────────┬─────────────┘     │
            │                  │                    │
            ↓                  │                    ↓
┌──────────────────────┐      │          ┌──────────────────────┐
│  Counterproliferation│      │          │    Threat reduction  │
│        policy        │      │          │         policy       │
└──────────────────────┘      ↓          └──────────────────────┘
                  ┌──────────────────────────┐
                  │    Deterrence strategy   │
                  └──────────────────────────┘

┌──────────────────────┐                  ┌──────────────────────┐
│ Contingencies, missions, │              │     Declaratory      │
│    and capabilities   │                 │        policy        │
└──────────────────────┘                  └──────────────────────┘

┌──────────────────────┐  ┌──────────────────────┐  ┌──────────────────────┐
│   Force structure    │  │  Plans, operations,  │  │   Safety, security,  │
│  and infrastructure  │  │      and C3a         │  │    and use control   │
└──────────────────────┘  └──────────────────────┘  └──────────────────────┘
```

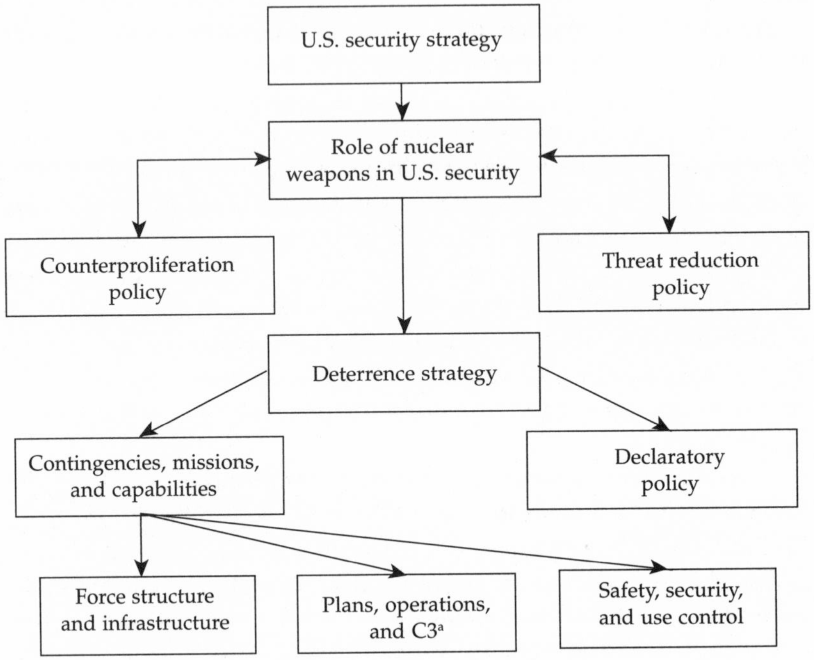

Source: Senate Committee on Armed Services, *Briefing on the Results of the Nuclear Posture Review*, 103d Cong., 2d sess., September 22, 1994, p. 6.

a. "C3" denotes command, control, and communications.

prevailed. For the air force and the strategic planning community in Washington and Omaha, in particular, the changes brought about under Secretary of Defense Richard Cheney and General Colin Powell already had stressed the system, albeit without overt or publicized signs of discord, and reforms were still in the process of implementation. Plans for the targeting and execution of forces, in any case, were and would remain the purview of experienced professionals. "We know how to produce nuclear war plans. We have the methodology, we can analyze damage expectancies," said one midlevel officer, who was infuriated by the intrusive approach of the recently appointed Clinton officials.[21] No matter what the changes in external threats being emphasized at the political level, nuclear planning was not an area for heavy-handed interference, especially by amateurs.

There were exceptions to this point of view among senior military officers. Admiral Owens, for one, is widely reported to have been a harsh critic of nuclear weapons and apparently expressed strong views in this regard over the course of the review.[22] In addition, General Butler, who was present for the early planning phases of the review until his retirement in early 1994, recently claimed that he pressed for major operational reforms and deeper reductions in nuclear forces, down to a level of 2,000.[23] Butler's early departure aside, neither Owens nor Butler is credited with very energetic efforts to challenge their colleagues in a way that would influence the outcome of the review. There was skepticism about it among career bureaucrats as well, including individuals who had witnessed these kind of bold initiatives before, usually undertaken early in new administrations before appointees have had a chance to become seasoned by the realities of government service.

Frank Miller, in particular, the respected Pentagon authority on nuclear issues who became Carter's principal deputy after serving in four previous administrations, had been part of many policy struggles between appointees and the established bureaucracy.[24] Miller saw himself as the new appointees' link to the institutional memory—and institutional minefields—that had to be considered before launching a challenge to the nuclear bureaucracy. Miller himself bore the scars of clashes between appointees and careerists and had learned how to be a "samurai bureaucrat" in the process, according to a colleague. As he saw it, he would help educate and protect his bosses, tempering their more brash tendencies while interpreting tasking orders in terms that the bureaucracy could understand.

Miller was more deeply skeptical of Soviet, now Russian, intentions than some members of the new administration seemed to be and was particularly concerned about unilateral U.S. concessions to Russia until the evidence for Russian conversion to democracy was more compelling. Miller had one basic metric for nuclear deterrence, the familiar axiom that U.S. nuclear forces were needed in quantities sufficient to hold at risk and destroy enemy nuclear launch sites. As long as Russian forces capable of attacking the United States were deployed and operational, there was no question but that the United States needed alert and highly capable forces for full target coverage. Russian rhetoric about peace and partnership or agreements signed but not yet fully implemented were simply not a sufficient basis for significantly deactivating or reducing U.S. capabilities.

Miller had helped spearhead the Bush administration's targeting review, including what he calls "a quiet revolution" in nuclear planning that resulted in a downscaling of the SIOP and provisions for adaptive targeting. The perception among some officials involved in the Bush review was that this exercise answered the question, How much is enough? even though this number has continued to change in response to policy directives (from 4,700 in 1992 to 3,500 in 1995 to 2,000–2,500 as of 1998). Consolidating the nuclear commands into a single entity under STRATCOM, Miller believed, finally created a coherent system to integrate doctrine, targeting, and force requirements. Not least among the factors driving his judgment was the degree to which he had earned a place at the table in the inner sanctum of the nuclear planning community, a hard-won victory that depended on enduring working relationships.[25]

In addition, Miller was not seized with the urgency expressed by Carter and some of his subordinates about the operational risks of the nuclear posture or the supposed pressure imposed on decisionmakers by a posture emphasizing the prompt launching of forces. He disagreed with Carter and others who argued that a president would be faced with a stark "use or lose" choice in crisis, precluding alternative options, being convinced that many of these problems had been solved in 1991.[26] Miller's conception of a revolution in nuclear operations achieved in the Bush administration did not track with the more radical ambitions of some of his new colleagues, one of whom caustically dismissed Miller's prior reforms as "an amelioration of evil."[27] What changes may have been made earlier were cosmetic, at best, according to critics. "These plans were just the old SIOP, doing everything we were doing before, but just smaller only because the Russian target base had shrunk."[28]

Despite Cheney's interventions in 1991 and the new directives he issued, the criteria for targeting continued to be based on the planning staff's notion of what was needed to destroy whatever adversaries most valued, from nuclear weapons to leadership to "other military targets." Target criteria still allowed for great latitude in interpretation, with target options for multiple weapons to be not just nuclear forces but also, for example, nuclear storage sites, petroleum facilities, and the manufacturing base. The category of war-supporting industry (which had in

44

previous plans allowed for such miscellaneous targets as shoe factories) were deemphasized somewhat but remained one of the priorities. As one participant summed it up, "Opponents of change defined deterrence as 'what has to be held at risk' in the target base, going after what the adversary values. If he values his grandma, we have to target grandmas."[29]

Miller and Carter in fact had different conceptions of the purpose of the nuclear posture review, according to several accounts. For Miller, this was an opportunity to analyze who the "bad guys and potential bad guys" were, to identify what the latter valued, and to determine accordingly what, if anything, needed to be changed in the existing plans to sustain a credible deterrent. The purpose was to identify a *deterrent* strategy for a new threat environment, not a new targeting strategy. That said, Miller carried out the directives issued by Carter to organize and manage the review process, albeit in a way that tried to harmonize the distinct points of view held by Carter and career professionals.

For Carter and others, the basic premises of a centralized nuclear attack plan not only were an atavism of the cold war but also posed new risks in light of emerging political and military conditions in Russia. At its core, the problem was that the United States and Russia maintained force structures that could not clearly survive an attack without being launched so promptly that both sides were operating in a hairtrigger scenario, a strategy rendered pointedly more dangerous by the fragile and worsening conditions in Russia. The message imparted by this posture, they argued, was not consistent with an environment in which the risk of deliberate attack was far less urgent than inadvertent or accidental launch prompted by miscalculation.[30] Deterrence would be far better served with smaller, survivable forces and operational guidelines that moved both sides away from a preoccupation with imminent or surprise attack.[31]

The Pentagon was thus about to launch a review of nuclear policy involving fundamental theological differences about nuclear weapons between appointees and career officials and even, in some cases, among appointees.[32] The basic character of deterrence was in dispute, a metaphor for broader disagreements over the utility of nuclear weapons after the cold war and even over the degree to which the Russian threat had actually changed. Two distinct conceptual frameworks were represented—and were bound to collide: a vision of nuclear security that deemphasized a reliance on targeting and prompt operations in favor

45

of "mutual assured safety" and cooperative denuclearization; and the contrasting view that the uncertain character of changes in Russia (and in the international system) compelled adherence to classic deterrence as well as the adoption of new nuclear options for emerging threats.

The Process

Questions drafted under Carter's direction were added to the agreed-on terms of reference to set the agenda for the individual working groups, each of which was given specific areas of inquiry: force structure and infrastructure; plans, operations, and command and control; counterproliferation policy; threat reduction policy; safety, security, and use control; contingencies, missions, and capabilities; and declaratory policy. Carter tasked the groups to consider issues well outside the norm, including the elimination of all prompt counterforce weapons, vastly reducing the alert level of U.S. and Russian forces, linking the U.S. nuclear force posture with third world incentives for proliferation, and even U.S. renunciation of the right to initiate the use of nuclear weapons. Carter was most preoccupied with promoting safety over promptness in the nuclear posture, pushing for ways to reduce the alert status of the two sides' forces and the de facto capability to launch forces in response to warning of an attack.

The working groups were provided with briefing materials to inform discussion and to help answer the questions posed to them. A stream of outside experts, some known for their less than orthodox views, were invited to give briefings. Several put forward arguments in favor of such major innovations as the United States taking all of its strategic forces off alert and the stopping of prompt counterforce targeting. Officials "gave a polite reception" to the outsiders, according to one account, or "looked puzzled beyond redemption," according to another.[33] Working group members tended to treat experts' articles and papers as obscure academic treatises, remote from the realities of operational planning. According to one participant, some of these were actually counterproductive. A briefing book provided by a Center for Strategic International Studies analyst presenting the case for policies of no first use, negative security assurances, and other steps for reducing nuclear dangers, for example, "just provided people with a concise list of what to argue against."[34]

The most important divisions in the Nuclear Posture Review were sparked by Carter's attempt to force the bureaucracy to develop options that, in his view, could harmonize U.S. operational policy and the criteria for force requirements in support of the stated declaratory doctrine of strict retaliation. If U.S. policy was to deter adversaries by maintaining forces capable of surviving and responding to an attack, according to this logic, it would follow that forces be made sufficiently survivable to ride out an attack and still be able to launch a devastating retaliatory blow—one that would preclude any perceived advantage to the aggressor. A stated policy of ride out, Carter argued, would eliminate the need for (and reduce the risk of) forces configured for rapid reaction and, as important, bring operational practices in line with the lessened risk of deliberate attack and the need to strengthen U.S.-Russian cooperation.

Force requirements would be planned accordingly, eliminating vulnerable systems that require prompt launch to survive (such as intercontinental ballistic missiles, or ICBMs) and discarding operational notions at odds with a policy of retaliation. Moving away from a posture relying on land-based missiles operating at "a constant alert rate of approximately 98 percent," which Chiles, the former STRATCOM commander, stated to be a requirement, implied a radical restructuring of forces and alert levels.[35] Aside from eliminating ICBMs altogether, Carter pushed the working groups to examine ways for the United States and Russia to remove warheads from missiles and to institute mutual inspections as a way to remove incentives for surprise or prompt attack. Such a force nevertheless would allow for a credible and survivable deterrent based on submarines and advanced bombers (along with improvements in command, control, communications, and intelligence, which would be essential) sufficient to deter or retaliate against any conceivable adversary.

The majority of career military and civilian officials involved in the review overwhelmingly opposed replacing or precluding existing options with either a policy of ride out or a policy to de-alert missile forces, whatever the perceived political logic. For some, any deviation from a posture that allowed for a variety of launch options, including massive and early launch if the situation warranted it, threatened the U.S. ability to respond to attacks and, by definition, weakened deterrence. Reserving a variety of launch options accepted the tension between the implied message imparted by the configuration of forces and the way a decision to launch would actually take place. As a former air force chief of staff explained, "there was . . . a very deliberate absence of policy. . . . The real expectation at SAC was that no president would 'launch-on-warning.' The assumption, though never stated as public policy, was that even with dual phenomenology [two separate indicators of impending attack], the warning would not be sufficiently convincing until the first impacts on U.S. soil. But, given those first impacts, it was also considered unlikely that any president [would] then continue to 'ride-out' a massive first strike." Opponents of the ride-out policy argued that deterrence would be damaged given "the concern over giving a potential attacker, no matter how remote the potential, the comfort of a formal U.S. ride-out policy."[36] As in many other instances, the logic hinged on heightening the uncertainty of enemies about U.S. plans, the opposite of the view that deliberately reducing Russia's uncertainty would enhance stability and increase prospects for cooperative nuclear reductions.

Determining what constituted a "requirement" was a central question raised in this discussion. Carter's view was that requirements should reflect what was needed to maintain a survivable force poised for retaliation. Opponents argued that nuclear force requirements had to be driven by what would best destroy particular target sets, particularly high-priority targets such as an enemy's forces. Although many senior officers had acknowledged well before the nuclear posture review that a successful strike against a wide range of Russian targets was increasingly implausible, the preparations for such operations remained vital to deterring enemies. One participant noted, "This leads to the paradox of force requirements being driven by the scenario of prompt response," even if such a contingency was understood to be remote.[37] Other proposals to change the character of targeting, as such—deemphasizing plans to hold nuclear forces at risk, for example, in favor of counter-military (conventional) forces—also met with skepticism.

The three major arguments against changing targeting priorities away from the other side's nuclear forces are that (1) holding an enemy's nuclear forces at risk has deterrent value, since it demonstrates that the United States could survive and respond to any conceivable attack—known as damage limitation, (2) the threat of attack on other forces or urban centers is not credible, and (3) a shift in targeting away from military assets—that is, targeting innocent civilians—would be seen as immoral. These standard rationales usually do not take into account the civilian casualties likely to be associated with any level of nuclear engagement and ascribe special importance to the perceived morality of a strategy aimed at forces rather than populations. It is generally acknowledged that a major nuclear exchange would result in thousands of civilian casualties, regardless of targeting doctrine, but the military-civilian distinction remains central to arguments against reducing nuclear forces below a certain threshold.[38]

Fundamental thinking about nuclear operations and the need for some significant element of forces to remain on alert had not changed profoundly since the 1980s. Nuclear forces were much diminished in number, but their configuration was believed by many, consciously or not, to require essential conformity with cold war arrangements. Each leg of the triad had to be preserved and options for continued modernization carefully protected. STRATCOM resisted, in particular, any move to eliminate the ICBM force. "That is something we at STRATCOM feel strongly about," said air force Lieutenant General Arlen D. Jameson, the command's deputy commander in chief, emphasizing the already diminished status of nuclear forces and cuts in the stockpile.[39] Already, alert levels had been reduced for bombers (although they could be reconstituted on alert in seventy-two hours), and missiles were ostensibly detargeted.

Further proposals for de-alerting, such as separating warheads from missiles as a way of increasing stability, according to this view, posed insurmountable operational problems that put deterrence at risk. In public testimony, Butler emphasized the limitations on secure storage of warheads removed from missiles, requiring that a significant portion of the U.S. missile force would have to be stored at sites distant from their delivery vehicles, which would require overland transportation. Logistics aside, the general was alluding to the more prevalent reason for opposition to de-alerting: the belief that it would degrade the operational readiness of nuclear weapons and thus undercut U.S. credibility. For some, Russian compliance with such a measure could not be fully verified, while U.S. compliance could invite opportunistic aggression.[40]

In addition to strategic policy, some of the questions concerned one of the most sensitive issues facing the administration: whether and how nuclear weapons could be used against nuclear and nonnuclear regional threats. The issue had been debated among officials in the previous administration, including Defense Secretary Cheney as part of the nuclear targeting review he initiated. Quasi-official reports stressing the need to devise nuclear plans for third world contingencies were released publicly, prompting media and public criticism. A study group commissioned by General Butler and chaired by Thomas Reed, secretary of the air force, released a report in late 1991 highlighting the risks of failing to prepare nuclear responses to nuclear, chemical, and biological threats from regional adversaries; included in the possible measures were the arming of expeditionary forces with low-yield, portable weapons.[41] Reed testified before the Congress in January 1992: "It is not difficult to entertain nightmarish visions in which a future Saddam Hussein threatens U.S. forces abroad, U.S. allies or friends, and perhaps even the United States itself with nuclear, biological, or chemical weapons. If that were to happen, U.S. nuclear weapons may well be a resource for seeking to deter execution of the threat"[42]

The Clinton administration distanced itself from many of these conclusions, deferring to the political sensitivities of the upcoming review conference on the Nuclear Non-Proliferation Treaty by reiterating the standing policy that the United States does not target nonnuclear countries. But the debate intensified internally, especially in light of continued tensions over the nuclear program in North Korea, which was precipitating a flurry of diplomatic and military threats against Pyongyang.

The Outcome

The bureaucratic arrangements set up to conduct the nuclear posture review were an early indication that the endeavor likely would fall short of its initial ambitions. In stark distinction from the reforms undertaken by Bush, the review was organized to delegate work to the Pentagon bureaucracy, particularly to midranking and even junior military officers and career bureaucrats, who formed the majority of the working group members. Many of the individuals had little background in nuclear issues, and few had any appreciation for or interest in the political dimensions of nuclear strategy. Like the Bottom-Up Review and the Quadrennial Defense Review that followed it, the Nuclear Posture Review was designed in a way that inhibited discussion of the broad dimensions of policy, with individual groups disaggregated by subject area, in an elaborate staffing scheme that operated without benefit of sustained senior leadership.

Some senior military officers and career officials appointed to oversee the effort not only were opposed to many of the policy departures being put forward by political appointees but also, as became increasingly obvious, were not supportive of the overall review process. The core leadership group, including Generals McCaffrey and Clark in particular, were adept at deflecting attention from proposals with which they disagreed and, according to one participant, "hopelessly outmatched Carter in the art of bureaucracy."[43] The prospects for a thorough review worsened when it became clear that few senior officials inside or outside the Pentagon wanted to be directly associated with the review. Aside from wanting to attend to more pressing and, to many, more interesting responsibilities, there was a growing reluctance to be part of deliberations in which controversy threatened to—or did—erupt publicly.[44] As mentioned earlier, Owens is said to have been vocal in his criticism of existing nuclear policies and even to have proposed some radical reforms of his own; but apparently he was not willing to fight for his views when he encountered opposition. Most important, the president and his close White House and cabinet advisers never indicated clearly that they had a stake in the outcome. A Pentagon official in favor of nuclear reforms alleges that "[Secretary of State Warren] Christopher was completely disengaged and [National Security Adviser] Anthony Lake was preoccupied."[45]

The enduring problem was that the working groups were simply ignoring Carter's tasking orders to come up with wide-ranging options. The groups continued instead to generate view graphs and analyses in support of the structure, doctrine, and force levels of the current posture, to go no lower than the limits set for START II, and to oppose consideration of other, even minor, innovations. Whether they had clear guidance and directives is open to question. As Carter became involved in competing policy priorities, including the denuclearization of the former Soviet republics, operational control for the working groups fell increasingly to Miller and other career and military officials. According to several accounts, Miller consistently worked to deflect some of the more unorthodox ideas being put forward by Carter, either by trying to persuade Carter of the inevitable backlash of moving too ambitiously or by recasting directives to blunt their predictably abrasive impact.

By January 1994, the working group that had been given the mandate to address the question, Why do we need nuclear weapons? briefed its results to Deutch. The conclusions not only championed the cold war status quo but were so pedestrian, according to one participant, that Carter declared the session "a disaster."[46] As one account describes it, "the working group envisioned a 21st-century nuclear force that looked a lot like the Cold War–era force, only smaller."[47] Carter took action, appointing two individuals on temporary assignment to the Pentagon to try to rescue the process: Steve Fetter, a University of Maryland professor trained in physics who was active in arms control debates, and Lieutenant Commander Leo Mackay, a naval officer who had written his Harvard doctoral dissertation on nuclear strategy under Carter's direction and was serving as Carter's military assistant. It was an unconventional solution, to say the least. Carter arranged for the two to receive the high-level clearances needed for full access to the relevant planning documents, in itself a bureaucratic precedent. According to Fetter, Carter then declared Fetter "in charge of organizing the next NPR briefings . . . but without ever telling anyone else that they should cooperate with or support me."[48] Miller, for example, was not informed by Carter and found out about the unorthodox arrangements "by accident," as he put it.[49]

Fetter and Mackay set about to construct alternative targeting strategies and force postures, conducting independent analyses of the assumptions being used to evaluate plans and requirements, from the calculation of force exchange ratios to the cost of alternative force configurations. They analyzed proposals for radical changes in detail, including, inter alia, postures operating with much smaller strategic forces, different targeting doctrines, a dyad with no land-based missiles, and the removal of remaining nuclear weapons from Europe. These proposals were then taken to the staffers in Miller's office (Nuclear Forces Policy) who were in charge of preparing the official briefing materials—the approved view graphs that would be used to present the arguments to Deutch and Owens. Fetter and Mackay encountered immediate resistance at the working level but were able to overcome initial objections by pulling rank. After each draft was produced, however, a small group convened in Miller's office to "haggle over the wording," as one put it. Although no proposed options were actually deleted at this point, one caustic critic alleged that "this was an opportunity for Frank to improve the 'pros' for his preferred [status quo] option, and the 'cons' for the new options."[50]

Even as the official working groups continued to meet, Carter arranged to present some of the findings of his "counter-review" to Deutch and Owens in two briefings between March and April 1994. The briefings to Deutch included an analysis of six options, ranging from a perfunctory discussion of the status quo, to eliminating the land-based leg of the triad, to a very low-level minimum deterrent force. The analysis presented detailed plans for the forces needed to fulfill deterrence requirements under different operational assumptions, including different ways to calculate damage expectancies and other planning criteria. The original mandate of the review was to explore these kinds of option, answering the basic question of how the nuclear force posture could fulfill strategic and political objectives with less risk, lower costs, and greater compatibility with changes in the threat environment.

Although there was brief discussion of the status quo option in these sessions, the core of the analysis tried to demonstrate empirically how a policy of prompt launch under alert conditions distorted the level of requirements well beyond what was needed for post–cold war deterrence. Even if unstated as a matter of policy, the emphasis on the ability to launch promptly, the briefers argued, created conditions that undermined the credibility of U.S. assurances to Russia that it would use nuclear weapons only in retaliation. The ambiguity of U.S. intentions reflected in the difference between stated policy and operational posture, they asserted, could prompt an adversary to strike first in a crisis for fear of having no retaliatory capability left after a U.S. strike.

The arguments in favor of a fully operational ride-out force were consistent with Carter's concerns about operational safety and supportive of a U.S. policy of retaliation. The core philosophy of the arguments emphasized the risks imposed by the disjuncture between a stated policy of retaliation and operational practices biased against riding out an attack. The long-standing schism between political assumptions about the utility of nuclear weapons and actual plans, to say nothing of the resulting inflation in force requirements, not only had lost any justification after the demise of the Soviet Union, it was argued, but also was increasingly counterproductive. It interfered with efforts to achieve agreements for greater force reductions and operational safety with Russia—measures needed to hedge against the more credible threat of a nuclear crisis precipitated by the collapse of the Russian government's increasingly tenuous political control.

The idea that ambiguity is a virtue for deterrence—a long-standing tenet of U.S. strategy—was presented in these briefings as detrimental to achieving greater stability with Russia. Also, the arguments were an obvious assault on the logic that was dominating the analysis of the working groups, which argued that deterrence was best served by keeping a variety of launch options and a triad of forces—which definitely included land-based missiles operating on high alert. The debate, in short, was a microcosm of the divergent perceptions of how to manage U.S.-Russian relations after the cold war as well as the relative utility of nuclear forces in a changed environment.

The second briefing to Deutch, scheduled for April 22, 1994, ultimately "triggered a revolt" in the Pentagon, according to Mackay.[51] Prior dissemination of Carter's briefing charts among the Joint Chiefs of Staff and the joint staff set off alarm bells when it was discovered that Carter would be presenting Deutch with proposals to drastically reduce or eliminate the ICBM force, to consider taking the ICBM force off alert, and even more radical proposals. Reacting to a leaked copy of Carter's briefing (or in actuality a copy of one of the several drafts circulating in the Pentagon), four deputy chiefs for operations and plans from each of the services sent a letter to Vice Admiral Richard Macke, joint staff director, objecting to Carter's freelance operation and insisting that the briefing be canceled.[52]

Only two of the options to be presented to Deutch had been vetted by the working groups, the officers complained, while any decision to eliminate ICBMs or to otherwise modify the triad had been vehemently opposed in the working groups. The Office of the Secretary of Defense, they charged, had violated the terms of the review by ignoring the duly appointed representatives of the Joint Chiefs, who were still meeting in the official process, and by putting forward its own options without adequate consultation. The OSD, moreover, was not authorized to do targeting analysis. Just the idea of "off-line" briefings were heresy to the military officers and career professionals, particularly based on analysis from subordinates who had been given access to planning documents and targeting data in violation of accepted protocol.

The letter, intended to prevent Carter from briefing Deutch and to force the review process back into the working groups, was leaked to the Congress. It surfaced on April 20, two days before the scheduled meeting with Deutch, during a Senate Armed Services Committee hearing receiving testimony from Admiral Henry Chiles, commander of the U.S. Strategic Command. Asked by Strom Thurmond (R-S.C.), the ranking minority member, if he supported the elimination of land-based missiles, Chiles assured the senator that no such proposal had been seriously entertained in the review working groups. To the contrary, he said, "ICBMs are necessary in our force of the future, and I believe we have argued that point within the Nuclear Posture Review." In the same hearing, Chiles also cautioned against a policy of riding out nuclear attacks, linking the danger of this posture to the threat of "rogue leaders in the world," who would no longer be deterred.[53] The hearing thus put the head of STRATCOM on record as opposing substantive changes in the force posture before the conclusion of the review.

These incidents escalated into opportunities for partisan attack against the Clinton administration. Four Republican senators sent a letter to the president objecting to Carter's attempts to evade the nuclear posture review process, for example: "It is our understanding that [despite the conclusion of the working group supporting START II force levels], a force structure recommendation that eliminates the land-based leg of the Triad is still being considered, and may be the preferred option of the NPR's chairman." The letter went on to emphasize the hazards of such a proposal, including the sudden vulnerability of the United States to a first strike: "Using only a handful of weapons, any nation with ICBM capability could mortally wound the U.S.'s ability to defend itself simply by attacking our bomber bases, submarine bases, and Command, Control and Communications centers." The letter notes that this threat would emerge not only from Russia but also from "China and other nations."[54]

Carter's second briefing to Deutch went forward despite objections. One participant claims that, during this session, Deutch found the case for eliminating ICBMs compelling. Concerns about operational doctrine aside, Deutch was reportedly attracted by the savings that would result from not having to rebuild the Minuteman III force, which otherwise would need investment for new motors and guidance packages over the next ten to fifteen years. Any moves in this direction, however, were apparently distracted by further opposition to Carter. The most dramatic showdown occurred in a meeting of regional commanders, initiated to "call Ash on the carpet," according to one report. The generals stated much the same objections as had been expressed in the letter to Macke but in a much more pointed and, some say, brutal way. The bottom line was that Carter had no authority to present options to the secretary of defense or to any other political appointee unless these proposals had been considered and approved by the working groups. Carter reportedly was visibly shaken and tried to reason with the officers, arguing that it is not appropriate for colonels and lower-level Pentagon personnel to craft U.S. national policy. The briefings with Deutch were exploratory: "They were just options," he was said to have argued in his defense. He had presented the full range of possibilities, including the status quo option, and had no intention of subverting the Joint Chiefs. His pleas were not persuasive. For the disaffected officers who hovered outside the door and gloated while the meeting was under way, Carter had finally been properly chastised.[55]

Watching Carter get dressed down may have given his critics cheap thrills, but it was not a good precedent for civil-military relations. Even if the political repercussions of conducting a "counter review" were predictable, this incident raised serious issues about the authority of appointed officials. Carter was designated the Office of the Secretary of Defense's overseer of the nuclear posture review. His mandate was to generate options for the nuclear posture for consideration by senior leaders. No one at higher political levels, however, defended Carter's right to carry out his study, even if it could be argued that it was the only way to implement directives from the secretary of defense in the face of determined bureaucratic roadblocks. One senior civilian official who was centrally involved questions whether there was any significance to these events. "We had to do this by consensus," he argues, "there's a difference between a breakdown of authority and abiding by the rules of consensus."[56] That said, it is not clear why appointees were given a mandate to conduct a policy review if they were not going to be granted the authority to carry it out. President Bush had given full support to his deputies (including Cheney, Powell, and National Security Adviser Brent Scowcroft) to override bureaucratic obstacles and implement directives known to have his full commitment. The outcome of a study of reforms of the nuclear posture conducted by consensus among midlevel officers and career officials, by contrast, was a preemptive fait accompli—a way to ensure ratification of the status quo.

In sharp contrast to numerous public and private accounts, another key participant has since disclaimed that there was ever any genuine intent to change the U.S. force posture or overall policy. According to this individual's current recollection, there was consensus among top officials as early as late 1993 that the international climate precluded consideration of any significant changes in the nuclear force posture. "It would have been idiotic to take unilateral reductions beyond START

II before getting START I implemented and START II ratified," he stresses, claiming that only "self-absorbed arms controllers and unilateral disarmers" ever argued to the contrary. "We always knew it was not the right time to change the force posture," not for reasons of domestic politics but because of "historical realities," including the confused conditions in Russia and the more immediate need to move forward with other initiatives, such as eliciting Ukrainian agreement for removing nuclear weapons from its soil.[57]

The review from that point became an exercise in face-saving, "slapping on a happy face" on what was left of this initiative, as another participant describes it.[58] The remaining discussion was highly circumscribed, focusing mostly on modest cuts unrelated to doctrine, such as reductions in Minuteman III missiles, from 500 to a level of 300–350, and limits on the number of B-52s and B-2 bombers. Further reductions were rejected pending Russian progress in arms reductions, while consideration of a no-first-use policy was put aside. A proposal to store nuclear warheads separately from ICBMs, supported by Carter and considered briefly as a possible initiative to be presented to Russian President Boris Yeltsin when he came to Washington for a summit in September, was opposed by the air force and languished.[59] And changes in the target base did not go much beyond those implemented by Cheney in 1992, a point emphasized subsequently by Deutch in congressional testimony. Most of the review's final deliberations were promptly leaked to congressional critics and thus were adjudicated in a highly charged political environment. A letter leaked to Congress in September from Chiles to Perry saying he could not support anything less than 500 ICBMs added to the pressure on Deutch and Perry to avoid further congressional controversies. Intense maneuvering and backpedaling continued until the day before the final results of the review were to be briefed to the president.[60]

In the end, Carter's office produced thirty-seven pages of charts and diagrams for public release (and a longer classified briefing), recommending that there be no significant changes in the nuclear weapons policies of Clinton's predecessor. Forces would go no lower than START II levels, nuclear weapons would be retained in Europe at current levels, and there would be no serious alteration in U.S. operational policies, including the policy of first use. Secretary Perry was provided with several rationales for the decision to avoid major departures from the past, including an apparent disparity in the pace of dismantling U.S.

and Russian forces mandated by START (which, it was alleged, could lead to U.S. "numerical inferiority") and the danger of a potential resurgence of an adversary "still armed with 25,000 nuclear weapons."[61] Intelligence assessments at the time examined the difficulties that Russia faced in keeping to the schedule for weapons dismantlement, noting economic and technical constraints and differences in the way Russia and the United States implement dismantlement procedures. There was no evidence of Russian efforts to deliberately avoid compliance.[62]

For all of its travails, the new policy approved by the president only trimmed the numbers of submarines and bombers and proclaimed a firm commitment to a "lead and hedge" strategy: to continue to pursue arms control negotiations and encourage Russia to ratify START II while retaining U.S. nuclear options should the cold war return. The hedge strategy required the United States to be able to deploy strategic warheads at a level almost double the START II limits (see table 3-1).[63] The review reaffirmed the central importance of retaining a triad of strategic forces based on "the leading edge of technology" and in sufficient numbers to "hedge against a reversal of reforms and the nuclear reductions process and a return to an authoritarian military regime in Russia hostile to the United States" as well as to provide for a reserve force in the event of nuclear aggression by a third party.[64] The effort to force consideration of reforms proved remarkable only in the degree to which it ratified a nuclear order that helped to stall the momentum of the Bush administration's initiatives. The irony was noted by one senior Bush official, who complained that the ambitious reforms in nuclear policies that Bush was able to achieve were overshadowed in ensuing deliberations. In the end, the outcome was in direct contradiction to Aspin's mandate, moving from "where do we go after START II," as he put it, to what do we do under the constraints of START I and II.

It is not clear exactly why or exactly when progress in START came to be seen as politically or substantively incompatible with more significant changes in U.S. nuclear forces, at least as a concern prompted by international developments. Many of the severe technical, political, and economic constraints on Russia that delayed START I implementation and that continue to impede START II ratification were recognized in 1994. The United States sought to assist Russian denuclearization and to reassure Russian politicians that the United States was no longer an adversary. The logic of hedging against fragile political conditions in Russia seemed to many to be counterintuitive; "if Russia is on the brink,

Table 3-1. *The Principal Results of the Nuclear Posture Review*

Force structure

Strategic forces
— Maintain single-warhead Minuteman III ICBMs
— Reduce Trident SSBN fleet from 18 to 14
— Modernize all with D-5 missiles
— Limit B-2 bombers with nuclear role to 20
— Cut B-52 bomber force from 94 to 66

Nonstrategic nuclear forces
— Maintain current level (490) of U.S. tactical nuclear weapons in Europe
— Eliminate nuclear weapons capability from U.S. Navy surface ships
— Retain nuclear cruise missile capability on submarines
— Retain dual-capable aircraft

Infrastructure requirements

Nuclear weapon capability maintenance
— Cease underground testing and fissile material production (develop stockpile surveillance engineering base; maintain capability to refabricate and certify weapon types in stockpile; maintain science and technology base)
— Ensure availability of tritium
— No new-design nuclear warhead production

Nuclear safety, security, and use control

Nuclear role in U.S. force structure
— Removed custody of nuclear weapons from U.S. ground forces
— Ceased deployment at sea of naval nonstrategic nuclear forces
— Removed strategic bombers from day-to-day alert

Safety of weapon systems
— Introduced coded control devices (permissive action links)
— Upgrade PALs on Minuteman III ICBMs and B-52 bombers

Stockpile measures
— Since 1988, total active stockpile cut by 59 percent; further total reduction of 79 percent by 2003 (strategic warheads reduced by 47 percent since 1988 and 71 percent by 2003; nonstrategic nuclear forces warheads cut by 90 percent; NATO stockpile cut by 91 percent)[a]
— Storage locations reduced by over 75 percent
— Personnel with access to weapons or control cut by 70 percent

Source: Senate Committee on Armed Services, *Briefing on the Results of the Nuclear Posture Review*, September 22, 1994, 103d Cong., 2d sess. (Government Printing Office, 1994).

a. Since the briefing was published, the end date for implementation of Phase II of Start II has been changed to 2007.

wouldn't it make more sense to move rapidly to remove as many weapons as possible?" asked a Pentagon official.[65]

Having questioned Russian motives in being slow to dismantle weapons in compliance with START I and having stressed the importance of U.S. nuclear weapons to hedge against Russia as a nuclear rival, the posture review weakened the political position of Russian supporters of START. The lead-and-hedge strategy proved in part to be a self-fulfilling prophesy, adding an irritant to U.S.-Russian relations and lending credibility to the anti-Western hawks in the Duma, who were resisting nuclear reductions as part of their strategy to discredit U.S. intentions. When the new study was presented to Russian leaders and military officers, first in New York and subsequently in Moscow, it met with overt hostility. For pro-Western politicians who had hoped the review would provide them with ammunition to prove that the United States was now a partner, it instead "provoked a sigh of relief on the part of those people who didn't believe our relations were changing," according to Duma member Alexei Arbatov.[66]

Could the United States have helped alleviate the pressures on Russia and achieved its own arms control objectives by proposing negotiations for START III or by other measures to reassure the Russian government, as are now being considered a few years later? Although the answer for many would be obviously yes, it was simply "out of the question," according to a key former official who played a major role in the review process. Despite repeatedly emphasizing that international realities precluded such actions, he asks incredulously, "Do you really think Clinton would have been reelected if he had moved, without START I or START II, to go unilaterally to START III?"[67] This explanation may seem valid to some, but it is also an affirmation of the importance of domestic political factors in setting the terms of the conclusions of the Nuclear Posture Review. It does not explain why the Pentagon chose to allocate funds only for a START II posture in its future-year defense plan, despite continued delays in Russian ratification, nor why it has as yet not formally allocated funds to maintain a START I force, a decision that reflects domestic budget priorities and the continued hope that the Russians will ratify START II in the future.[68] It also does not explain why, three years after presenting the Nuclear Posture Review, Secretary of Defense Perry decided to offer the Russians a "framework" agreement for lower force levels even as U.S.-Russian relations were in decline and Russian rhetoric about the importance of nuclear weapons far more prominent.

For all of its initial and still potential promise, much of the arms control agenda that President Clinton inherited from his predecessor changed from a signal of far-reaching accommodation between former antagonists to contention, both international and domestic. By 1997, the political logic of the review—that the United States should make no further concessions to Russia because this would be taken as a sign of weakness—evolved into a discomforting perception that the Duma "has veto power over U.S. defense priorities," according to an adage now used by a broad range of military and private critics.[69] The executive branch currently maintains the view that Russian actions necessarily determine the future, a hedge against potential congressional criticism, perhaps, as much as a prudent military decision. As Stephen S. Rosenfeld noted after interviewing Secretary of Defense William Cohen:

> With the ending of the Cold War, the nature of the nuclear dilemma changed from the possibility of a general war to the possibility of accidental launch or rogue attack. Some believe the change opened the way to a wholesale revision of the American nuclear posture: taking all warheads off virtual hair-trigger alert, shrinking the arsenal swiftly toward zero weapons, ending the strategy of threatening massive nation-destroying retaliation and agreeing not to use nuclear weapons first.
>
> From an interview I had with Defense Secretary William Cohen . . . however, it is clear that hopes for these sorts of sweeping change have no home in the Clinton administration . . . for now we are, and for many years will be, ready however improbably to fight Russia or China or a rogue or terrorist in the instant massive Cold War way.[70]

No one disputes the uncertainty of conditions in Russia or in the international environment and the need to plan for adverse developments. The question of whether and what kind of nuclear deterrence policies may be effective or useful in containing incipient nuclear dangers, however, has still not been fully analyzed at senior levels. The challenges posed by the disintegration of the Russian military establishment, the political ascendance of Russian hard-liners who oppose accommodation with the West, and stepped-up Russian nuclear operations aimed at its neighbors cannot be managed by U.S. preparations for strategic nuclear operations; the connection is remote and, some argue, counterproductive. In relying on visions of Russia as a potential cold war enemy, however, the nuclear posture review turned away from addressing such challenges in favor of policies that hark back to a more familiar past.

A failure to ratify START II and to move forward with START III, which may be an increasingly plausible outcome, could have a chilling effect on all aspects of U.S.-Russian cooperation and could preclude any further progress toward reducing nuclear danger. The reaffirmation of nuclear weapons by both sides, in turn, could presage a change in the politics of proliferation, undercutting the viability of cooperative denuclearization agreements and rendering meaningless the pledges made by the nuclear powers to reduce reliance on nuclear weapons as part of the global nonproliferation bargain. According to one pessimistic commentator, "The clay of history is beginning to harden again."[71]

Nuclear Deterrence in the Third World and the Africa Nuclear Weapons–Free Zone Treaty

THE PROLIFERATION OF WEAPONS of mass destruction did not command the attention it deserved from policymakers during the cold war. It was commonly believed that fledgling third world arsenals would never pose a military threat that the West could not deter or counter with far superior forces. The great powers tended to ignore the security agendas of third world nations, assuming that the latter would conform to international norms banning the acquisition or use of nuclear or other unconventional weapons—or, if found to be in violation, that they could be readily induced to stop.[1] Proposals from states that supported nonproliferation, moreover—calling on the nuclear-armed members of the Nuclear Non-Proliferation Treaty to cut their arsenals, to stop developing and testing new weapons under a Comprehensive Test Ban Treaty, or to formally forswear the first use of nuclear weapons against nonnuclear states—typically were dismissed as unduly imposing on the force plans and modernization objectives of the established nuclear powers.

The 1968 Nuclear Non-Proliferation Treaty, however, rested on an essential bargain between the five nuclear weapons states (the United States, the Soviet Union, France, Britain, and China) and the nonnuclear weapons states, in which the latter agreed not to acquire nuclear weapons in return for a pledge from the nuclear powers "to pursue negotiations in good faith on effective measures relating to cessation of the

63

nuclear arms race at an early date and to nuclear disarmament, and on a Treaty on general and complete disarmament under strict and effective international control."[2] In four review conferences on the implementation of the treaty held every five years since 1975, the failure to achieve critical steps toward this objective—including a comprehensive test ban, or a ban on the production of weapons-grade fissile material—underscored the criticism among key states that the nonproliferation regime was discriminatory. This was a source of growing divergence between the nuclear and nonnuclear states about the legitimacy and utility of the treaty as a whole.

Pressure mounted on the Clinton administration in 1994 to devise a diplomatic agenda to elicit international support for the extension of the Nuclear Non-Proliferation Treaty, to be decided at the final review conference scheduled for April 1995. U.S. policy was that the treaty should be extended indefinitely and without conditions, an assertion of its importance to U.S. interests in promoting global nonproliferation norms. The linkage between the policies of the nuclear powers and the endurance of the regime became a more important and controversial consideration. The legitimacy of the treaty was increasingly under assault by influential countries such as Japan and Sweden as long as the United States and the other acknowledged nuclear powers continued to emphasize the importance of nuclear forces to their own security.[3]

Before and during the May 1995 Review and Extension Conference for the treaty, a number of countries that are part of the nonaligned movement, including Egypt and Indonesia, indicated that they would oppose extension of the treaty "indefinitely and without condition"—the U.S. position—absent clear pledges from the nuclear powers that they were committed to a specific agenda of nuclear disarmament. In addition to disaffection about the failure to embrace and implement the goal of elimination of nuclear weapons as called for under article 6, a number of key members raised the issue of security assurances. Selling the U.S. position internationally fell to Ambassador Thomas Graham, an official at the U.S. Arms Control and Disarmament Agency who had more than two decades of experience in arms control diplomacy. His job was seen by some as having one simple objective: to persuade enough countries to vote with the United States to ensure a clear majority.

The achievement of this objective involved a complex diplomatic agenda and repeated visits to governments around the world, a challenge managed by Graham with little involvement at more senior levels in the White House (or even at the State Department) until much later in 1994. Graham issued pledges to various states to help induce their cooperation, including a reaffirmation of the Clinton administration's commitment to a comprehensive test ban, negative security assurances, and exhortations about how the United States was eager to pursue a course of disarmament leading to the eventual elimination of nuclear weapons.

While Graham was championing the U.S. commitment to the treaty's obligations, the Pentagon planning was proceeding behind the scenes to consider the expansion of nuclear missions for regional contingencies. The utility of nuclear weapons to deter the use of third world nuclear and other weapons of mass destruction had been a subject of growing interest within the nuclear planning establishment well before the Clinton administration took up the issue. Analysis of nuclear options against third world aggressors emerged from targeting reviews conducted by the air force and the Strategic Air Command even before the war against Iraq. The Nuclear Weapons Employment Policy formulated in early 1991 and issued in 1992 under Secretary of Defense Cheney formalized procedures for nuclear operations against countries with the potential to develop weapons of mass destruction.[4] The consolidation of strategic nuclear forces under STRATCOM in 1992 also helped advance planning innovations to allow for nuclear forces to be flexibly and rapidly retargeted against "spontaneous threats that defy precise preplanning" as well as to add new regional targets to existing plans.[5] Nuclear adversaries other than Russia, including China and, more recently, rogue states with incipient nuclear capabilities, are covered by a strategic reserve force, which can cover an estimated 1,000 targets. The original rationale for the reserve force was to deter any nuclear adversary from seeking advantages after the United States had engaged in a nuclear conflict with Russia—a postattack scenario. The limited and selected attack options attached to the reserve force allow for rapid targeting and employment against regional adversaries.[6]

The design and integration of new nuclear options was well along in 1993, including the preparation of so-called silver books (strategic installation list of vulnerability effects and results), which prepared plans to launch military strikes against command centers and the stockpiles and production facilities of weapons of mass destruction in Libya, Iran, Iraq, and North Korea.[7] As General Lee Butler, commander of STRATCOM, saw it, the design of small nuclear options that could be retargeted quickly as the need arose would bring nuclear weapons into closer conformity with conventional forces and make their potential utility on the battlefield more credible.

The restructuring of SAC into STRATCOM transferred responsibility for planning regional nuclear options from the regional commanders to STRATCOM, allowing it to take over target planning for strategic and nonstrategic forces against states with weapons of mass destruction. Using adaptive planning and the reserve force, STRATCOM could implement a variety of attack options against regional threats in a matter of hours.[8] In 1994, Admiral Henry Chiles emphasized that new challenges would require greater speed and flexibility in planning operations: "In this changed environment, STRATCOM can no longer rely on a Cold War SIOP that takes 18 months to build. Instead, STRATCOM is developing an adaptive planning process to produce a variety of options for crisis response. The goal is greater adaptability and responsiveness to reduce the time necessary to provide the President with viable options. Hence, STRATCOM is modernizing the Strategic War Planning System with hardware and software upgrades. When *completed by 1999*, this system will enable STRATCOM to plan force employment options more rapidly in response to global contingencies."[9] It is noteworthy that the effort to integrate flexible planning options was still in gradual evolution six years after Major General Richard Goetze's categorical statement in 1988 that the traditional SIOP is "a thing of the past."[10]

Advances in conventional technologies and, in principle, the ability to plan small-scale nuclear strikes blurred the distinction between conventional and nuclear operations, a practical departure from the apocalyptic vision of nuclear engagement that has long dominated popular perceptions. Butler made efforts in 1993 to consolidate the conventional targeting of weapons of mass destruction under STRATCOM, which he argued had the requisite intelligence and planning capabilities to devise flexible options on short notice. He met strong resistance from the services, however, especially the regional commanders in Europe and the Pacific, even though existing arrangements among the regional commanders in chief made prompt and coordinated targeting extremely difficult. The Office of the Secretary of Defense (OSD) ceded to the prerogatives of regional commanders to create their own plans but without resolving how coordination among STRATCOM and the commands would be managed in a crisis.[11]

A consensus was growing in the planning community that, whether or not the United States would launch nuclear strikes against a non-nuclear adversary, it was important to retain the ability to threaten nuclear use as part of a robust deterrent. Opposition to proposals later raised in the nuclear posture review to discard first use in U.S. doctrine was well entrenched among senior officials and military officers. It was increasingly justified by reference to the growing regional threat beginning in the late 1980s. In 1991, Butler assured members of Congress that, although the United States would be unlikely to initiate nuclear attacks against the Soviet Union, "I don't know that there would be a great deal to be gained . . . by assuring some potential adversary, not necessarily the Soviet Union, . . . who has access to and a penchant to use biological or chemical weapons, to give them the absolute assurance that we would never use nuclear weapons first."[12] The concept of nuclear deterrence was expanded to not only the deterrence of attack but also the acquisition and development of such capabilities. U.S. nuclear forces would be now be used, according to Butler, to deter any "potentially hostile country that has or is seeking weapons of mass destruction."[13]

Studies have been commissioned by U.S. nuclear planners since 1991 to analyze nuclear weapons after the cold war, such as the Reed report, which outlines the need to expand the role of nuclear missions against regional adversaries, including, inter alia, a new SIOP to allow for a nuclear expeditionary force with "a handful of weapons, on alert, day to day" to use against China and other third world states.[14] A study issued by the navy in 1992 (known as STRATPLAN 2010) draws similar conclusions for naval strategy, including a nuclear reserve force with low-yield weapons, "providing a wider range or targeting options for maintaining a credible nuclear deterrence in the new world order."[15] An official publication put out in 1993 by the Joint Chiefs of Staff also defines the role of strategic forces as including regional and nonnuclear contingencies: "the fundamental purpose of U.S. nuclear forces is to deter the use of weapons of mass destruction [WMD]. . . . Deterrence of the employment of enemy WMD, whether it be nuclear, biological, or chemical, requires that the enemy leadership believes the United States has both the ability and will to respond promptly and with selective responses that are credible (commensurate with the scale or scope of enemy attacks and the nature of U.S. interests at stake) and militarily effective."[16] It was not until later in the 1990s that such discussions moved from intense secrecy to more open debate.

In the aftershock of Operation Desert Storm, the redefinition of proliferation from a diplomatic priority to an urgent military priority became a central preoccupation of policymakers as well. In a February 1992 report entitled "An Approach to Sizing American Conventional Forces in the Post-Soviet Era," Les Aspin, chairman of the House Armed Services Committee, argues that "regional aggressors" were the "main threat driver" in the post–cold war world. Aspin describes Saddam Hussein as "the very model of a modern, post-Soviet regional despot," noting that "he made an unprovoked military attack on his neighbor, he was in hot pursuit of nuclear weapons, he used terrorism to advance his ends, and he kept his own people in check by totalitarian means."[17] Aspin accordingly created what he called a "threat yardstick" to determine how other rogue states measured up to Saddam Hussein in terms of potential offensive force; the unit of measurement was the "Iraqi equivalent." Iran, Syria, Libya, North Korea, China, and Cuba were cited as meeting this measurement, and they quickly became synonymous with the term *rogue* (see figure 4-1). The report was a perfect merging of cold war and post–cold war security analysis: a pseudo-empirical assessment of a composite threat, based on the size or character of weapons arsenals or potential weapons arsenals, which belied the heterogeneity and complexity of the countries involved.

It was quickly concluded that this is not the kind of threat that should be left to the State Department or the United Nations. Without a devastating war, Iraq would have needed just a few more months to change history. Aspin spoke to the graduating class of MIT in 1992, just before his appointment as President Clinton's secretary of defense: "Consider what would have happened in Operation Desert Storm had Saddam Hussein's nuclear program produced a half dozen nuclear weapons— usable nuclear weapons—prior to 1990. Even if he had no delivery system to get to the United States, suppose he could hit Tel Aviv, Riyadh, or Ankara? How would that have affected our ability to conduct that kind of conventional military operation? The outcome may have been the same, but I am not sure."[18] The notion that the United States would have been unable to assemble a credible military coalition to deter or defeat a nuclear-armed, or even a chemically armed, Iraq took hold and soon became conventional wisdom. Compared to the vast nuclear forces and threat of aggression by a superpower that informed cold war de-

Figure 4-1. *Countries with Programs for Developing Weapons of Mass Destruction, in Place, Probable, and Possible*[a]

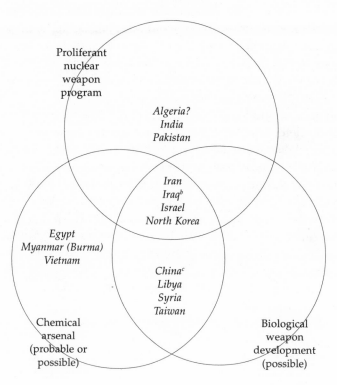

Source: Reproduced from Office of Technology Assessment, "Proliferation of Weapons of Mass Destruction: Assessing the Risks," August 1993, p. 15.

a. During special hearings convened by a House subcommittee in 1993, R. James Woolsey, former director of the Central Intelligence Agency, put forward an estimate still accepted today, which stressed that "over twenty-five countries, many of them hostile to the United States and its allies, may now have or may be developing nuclear weapons," and that "more than two dozen" had programs to develop arsenals of chemical weapons. These estimates include any country thought to be technically capable of assembling such weapons, whether they are involved in such activities or not. *Hearings before the Subcommittee on International Security, International Organizations and Human Rights: U.S. Security toward Rogue Regimes*, 103d Cong., 1st sess. (Government Printing Office, 1994).

b. Iraqi programs reversed by the United Nations.

c. China is an acknowledged nuclear weapons state.

terrence, Iraq raised the specter of a small country that, with just a few crude warheads and ballistic missiles, could paralyze the resolve of the international community.

Why would such a nation not fear devastating nuclear retaliation? Aspin explained this phenomenon based on the proposition that, "in this new world, nuclear deterrence may not always work." The Soviet

Union, poised for ready annihilation of the West, was an "ideologically hostile, aggressive adversary," but its government was rational and predictable. The Kremlin recognized that a nuclear attack upon the United States or its armed forces would be suicidal in the certainty of an overwhelming retaliation. This new class of states, however, are said to be something altogether different. "Will our nuclear adversaries always be rational, or at least operate with the same logic as we do?" Aspin asked. "We can't be sure."

Many policymakers agreed, lending impetus to the notion of states that are "undeterrable" and cannot be expected to behave like the Soviets. The belief that rogue states are inherently bellicose and have a higher tolerance for war and casualties invokes perceptions of the Soviet Union that were popular during the 1970s and 1980s and that persist in some form today. Richard Pipes, for example, an academic Soviet specialist who served as a member of an official study group known as Team B (which repudiated Carter-era intelligence estimates of the Soviet threat and rejected the logic of arms control negotiations) in the 1970s and briefly in the Reagan White House, argued that it was in the Russian character to believe that all war, including nuclear war, was winnable. "The Soviet ruling elite regards conflict and violence as natural regulators of all human affairs: wars between nations, in its view, represent only a variant of wars between classes." Pipes was persuaded that the behavior of the Soviet leadership was driven by their unique Russian peasant heritage, which "taught by long historical experience that cunning and coercion alone ensured survival."[19] Pipes' candid impression of the "Soviet character" was much more stark than those of his colleagues, but more understated variations were widely accepted. A former commander of SAC, for example, described his and his colleagues' attitudes about the Soviets in the 1970s in an interview in December 1997. Detailed to the strategic arms limitation talks in 1974 as an air force representative, he "like many of his colleagues . . . viewed the negotiations as a game with only one sure winner: the Soviet Union, a country he believed had an insatiable urge for aggression."[20]

In the aftermath of the cold war, policymakers seemed to almost lament the loss of their predictable former adversary. "When we faced the former Soviet Union, we had a clear understanding of what it would take to deter adventurism by Brezhnev or Khrushchev," observed Representative Doug Bereuter (R-Nebr.). "It seems more difficult to deter

Saddam Hussein or Qaddafi."[21] One analysis of public opinion data notes that "the ideological struggle [of the cold war], with its clearly defined boundaries of dispute and neatly categorized allies and adversaries, had been replaced by a much more amorphous, confusing and unpatterned array of potential threats characterized by ethnic, cultural or economic struggles."[22] The most common popular view of a rogue is the stereotype of the Muslim suicide bomber, a threat that has found great resonance among publics and policymakers. References to "political Islam" as a virulent strain of anti-Western and aggressive ideology increasingly appear in official and expert debate. As a former high-ranking government official summarizes it: "If a group of Iranian mullahs one day has a very long-range ballistic missile—and decides that not only they but all their countrymen can go to heaven if they just launch a nuclear weapon at the 'Great Satan'—that's not the kind of people deterrence would work against."[23]

Beginning in the early 1990s, several respected foreign affairs experts articulated similar themes. In 1993, for example, Samuel Huntington argued that conflicts among nations would not be ideological or economic in nature in the post–cold war world but rather that "the dominating source of conflict will be cultural" and that the "fault lines between civilizations will be the battle lines." Conflict between the West and the third world (particularly, the "Islamic" and "Confucian" countries) was said to be the preeminent risk. The globalization of ideas and habits that Huntington deemed Western, such as democracy, human rights, and free market economics, was said to be viewed by many non-Western nations as an assault upon their indigenous values. Trumpeted by Western liberals as a harbinger of an increasingly integrated and peaceful world, globalization for Huntington instead prompted a resurgence of aggressive nationalist ideologies, ranging from fundamentalist Islam to militant Russian pan-Slavism. Huntington also addressed weapons of mass destruction in this context, arguing that nuclear, chemical, and biological weapons, along with ballistic missiles, were bound to be viewed by emerging aggressors "as the potential equalizer of superior Western conventional power." To those non-Western countries resisting the forces of global integration, international organizations, including nonproliferation regimes, were simply tools to promote Western dominance and deprive non-Western states from achieving parity with the West.[24]

Although Huntington was criticized for his views by a variety of commentators, notions similar to his have seeped into assumptions guiding current policy. Huntington's rhetorical excesses about incompatible civilizations have been rejected, but the underlying rationales may differ more in nomenclature than in substance. Some administration officials, notably Anthony Lake, the national security adviser, sought to distance themselves from Huntington's thesis. In a speech in 1993, Lake asserted that it was wrong to assume that democratic ideals would be "embraced only by the West and rejected by the rest." Politics and economics, said Lake, are not shaped by "culture." Later, however, Lake seemed to accept a version of the thesis he decried, arguing that the expansion of democratic ideals was creating a group of "backlash states," whose resistance was driven not by their ethnicity or religion but by a shared political culture of authoritarianism, which posed a unique threat to the United States in the post–cold war era.[25] "Such reactionary, 'backlash states' are more likely to sponsor terrorism and traffic in weapons of mass destruction and ballistic missile technologies. They are more likely to suppress their own people, foment ethnic rivalries and threaten their neighbors."

That the "threat of the unknown" posed by hostile third world states is more unsettling than an enemy superpower capable of annihilating Western society is a perception now fully integrated into official policy statements and planning documents. For example, the Department of Defense's Quadrennial Defense Review (QDR) issued on May 19, 1997, states:

> Indeed, U.S. dominance in the conventional military arena may encourage adversaries to use . . . asymmetric means to attack our forces and interests overseas and Americans at home. That is, they are likely to seek advantage over the United States by using unconventional approaches to *circumvent* or *undermine* our strengths while *exploiting* our vulnerabilities. Strategically, an aggressor may seek to avoid direct military confrontation with the United States, using instead means such as terrorism, NBC [nuclear, biological, and chemical] threats, information warfare, or environmental sabotage to achieve its goals. If, however, an adversary ultimately faces a conventional war with the United States, it could also employ asymmetric means to delay or deny U.S. access to critical facilities; disrupt our command, control, communications and intelligence networks; deter allies and potential coalition partners from supporting U.S. intervention; or inflict higher than expected U.S. casualties in an attempt to weaken our national resolve.[26]

A Military Solution to Proliferation?

A critical part of the mandate of the nuclear posture review was to examine the role of nuclear weapons to deter some of these new regional adversaries. Revelations that Iraq and North Korea, both Nuclear Non-Proliferation Treaty signatories, had covertly acquired nuclear weapons technologies made the necessity of strengthening and enforcing international norms against nuclear proliferation all the more urgent. For many, the failure of the International Atomic Energy Agency (IAEA) to detect these programs was an indictment of the nuclear nonproliferation regime and its complex architecture of consensual agreements. That Western industrial countries, wittingly or otherwise, had been providing Iraq with technologies for developing weapons of mass destruction, that the international community never accorded the IAEA the authority or resources to conduct effective inspections of suspect programs, or that the intelligence community had not accorded a high priority to either Iraq or North Korea did not distract attention from the more compelling perception that new means of coercion were vitally needed.

Growing doubts within the national security community about the reliability of diplomatic arrangements lent an impetus to development of new military options for regional contingencies. With an eye toward potential third world aggressors, this "counterproliferation" initiative was an attempt to combine regional security strategies, deterrence, power projection, intelligence collection, and defenses into a single mission.[27] Although officials emphasized its focus on advanced conventional forces and defenses against weapons of mass destruction, the initiative was immediately perceived by some U.S. experts—and also internationally—as a plan to develop credible and, many believed, preemptive nuclear options for post–cold war challenges. In fact, the program includes precision-strike weapons for attacking military targets in proliferant countries; "detection and attack capabilities" for the destruction of installations that are hardened and underground; defenses against chemical and biological weapons; special operations forces; tactical antisatellite technologies run by the U.S. Army; and emergency preparedness and response, a broad category of programs to defend against nonconventional terrorist attacks.

Still, the reactions of NATO allies to briefings in 1994 about this counterproliferation initiative were extremely negative, in deference to the sensitivities of the upcoming Nuclear Non-Proliferation Treaty conference and the allies' preference for diplomatic over military approaches to nonproliferation. The reaction among regional powers was even more antagonistic. Rajiv Gandhi, for example, president of the All India Congress Committee, argued that a shift in U.S. policy to use nuclear weapons against a nonnuclear weapons state would deprive India of "any option but to convert its nuclear weapons capability into nuclear weapons capacity."[28]

The Nuclear Posture Review working group that examined regional missions for nuclear forces focused on the adequacy of U.S. military responses to not only the threat of nuclear proliferation but also the threat of chemical and biological proliferation, given the absence of commensurate U.S. chemical and biological capabilities. The key questions were whether conventional forces were "good enough" to deter unconventional threats and, if not, how nuclear weapons could best be configured to fill the gap.[29] Framing the issue in this way reinforced a central tenet in U.S. strategy going back to the 1950s: that nuclear weapons can make up for shortfalls in conventional weapons. This belief has coexisted with a contradictory legacy of the insurmountable operational challenges that commanders have encountered in trying to develop credible nuclear war plans, especially at the tactical level, to say nothing of political constraints on nuclear use. Once again, the challenge was to demonstrate how advances in technology—from low-yield "mininukes" to so-called high-powered radio frequency bombs (nuclear weapons designed to incapacitate enemy communications)—could make nuclear weapons demonstrably useful in limited engagements, including against hardened installations in states with illicit weapons programs.[30]

Despite the diplomatic sensitivity of contemplating nuclear strikes against new states (and despite representatives of the nuclear posture review issuing quite different statements to foreign governments), the tasking to come up with regional military options in the nuclear posture review overwhelmed the seriousness of directives to examine whether the United States could move to a policy of no first use. Renouncing the right to use nuclear weapons first, it was quickly concluded, would encourage rather than discourage aggression and proliferation among determined regional adversaries

Although they were based on scant and sometimes contradictory intelligence and expert reports, assessments of the coalition victory against Iraq helped legitimate the importance of nuclear threats in deterring Saddam Hussein from launching chemical and perhaps biological weapons against Western forces and allies. This interpretation remains controversial. A 1991 letter from President Bush and delivered by Secretary of State James A. Baker to Iraqi Foreign Minister Tariq Aziz, stating that the United States was ready to use "all means available" to retaliate against Iraq in the event of chemical use, has been portrayed by many experts as the reason that Iraq did not use chemical weapons.[31] Subsequent corroboration of this view was offered by an Iraqi defector, one of Saddam Hussein's sons-in-law, who left Iraq briefly in 1994 (he returned to Baghdad and was executed shortly thereafter). However, the preponderance of intelligence analyses that have been made public conclude that Iraq had not yet tested or mated operational missiles with chemical warheads and that Iraq may have been as much technically as politically constrained. An analysis conducted by a former head of Israeli counterintelligence also concluded that a decision to avoid the escalation of the conflict was inconsistent with Saddam Hussein's long-standing strategy, which is biased toward "going for broke" rather than calculated brinksmanship, especially under pressure.[32]

By mid-1994, intensifying tensions with North Korea over its nuclear program and the continued intransigence of Iraq in resisting United Nations inspections helped fuel perceptions that diplomatic arrangements were inadequate against rogue regimes and that military contingencies should be considered. Press reports in March 1994 that the Pentagon was changing long-standing U.S. policy not to target nonnuclear states forced the administration to deny this publicly.[33] "The NGOs [nongovernmental organizations] went ballistic," according to a National Security Council official, "and we were forced to kick the can."[34] The extension conference for the Nuclear Non-Proliferation Treaty imposed political discipline on the review process, at least temporarily. Robert Bell, senior director for defense policy and arms control on the National Security Council, cautioned colleagues to constrain their debate until after April 1995, when the treaty would presumably be concluded and serious consideration of nuclear missions taken up again. The nuclear posture review was duly silent on the subject of regional targeting.

By late 1994, U.S. officials, including the president, began to recognize that gaining majority support for a treaty extension, indefinitely and without conditions, was not guaranteed. Finally joining Ambassador Graham's efforts, the White House undertook a concerted strategy to persuade states to extend the treaty "indefinitely and without conditions," pledging U.S. leadership on behalf of a series of disarmament measures, including a commitment to achieve a comprehensive test ban by 1996 and a ban on the production and stockpiling of weapons-usable fissile materials. On March 1, 1995, the president gave a speech at the Washington-based Nixon Center for Peace and Freedom, calling for the nuclear weapon states "to pursue nuclear arms control and disarmament."[35] The original draft of the speech had Clinton calling for the "eventual elimination of nuclear weapons," consistent with article 6 of the treaty, but these words were deleted in response to opposition from individuals at the Pentagon.[36]

On April 5, 1995, the day before the conference began, the president issued a statement formally reinforcing long-standing U.S. policy to forswear nuclear targeting of nonnuclear states that are parties to the Nuclear Non-Proliferation Treaty. In carefully crafted diplomatic parlance, the statement said the following: "The United States reaffirms that it will not use nuclear weapons against any non-nuclear-weapon States Parties to the Treaty on the Non-Proliferation of Nuclear Weapons except in the case of an invasion or any other attack on the United States, its territories, its armed forces or other troops, its allies, or on a State towards which it has a security commitment, carried out or sustained by such non-nuclear-weapon State in association or alliance with a nuclear-weapon State."[37] Secretary of State Warren Christopher, who delivered the statement, added, "It is the administration's view that the national statements being issued by all five NPT nuclear-weapon states, their co-sponsorship of a Security Council resolution on security assurances which is under consideration in New York, and the common negative security assurance achieved by four of the five together comprise a substantial response to the desire of many NPT non-nuclear-weapon states for strengthened security assurances. This outcome reinforces the international nuclear proliferation regime and deserves the support of all NPT parties."[38] Taken together, the steps to shore up support for the Nuclear Non-Proliferation Treaty committed the United States to policies that renounced further nuclear modernization and that codified so-called negative security assurances.

The conciliatory climate and the success of the treaty extension conference notwithstanding, plans for regional nuclear operations increasingly dominated the internal security debate in the administration, especially in the Pentagon. For many who had been involved in the nuclear posture review, conventional forces were perceived as insufficient to deter rogue states from either acquiring or using weapons of mass destruction, to destroy the hardened underground bunkers being built to hide covert programs, or to protect U.S. territory or U.S. troops deployed overseas. The parallel efforts of diplomats and nuclear planners to design new approaches to combat proliferation increasingly were at odds, embodied in the conflicting agendas of the Nuclear Non-Proliferation Treaty and the move to incorporate nonnuclear states in nuclear targeting plans.

The Pelindaba Agreement

The administration did not fully join the debate, however, until early 1996, after the successful conclusion of the Africa Nuclear Weapons–Free Zone (ANWFZ) Treaty. This agreement among forty-three African states obligates nuclear states, under Protocol I, not to use or threaten to use nuclear weapons against any African state that is also a party to the treaty. The Pelindaba agreement, named after the town in which South Africa conducted its covert nuclear program until the program's termination by President Nelson Mandela, originated as a call by eight African countries in 1960 in the United Nations to respect Africa as a nuclear weapons–free zone. Reinvigorated after the election of President F. W. de Klerk in 1989, the final treaty was concluded in late 1995 and its protocol presented for signature to the nuclear powers. According to several accounts, the agreement caught senior-level U.S. officials completely by surprise. One White House official said his initial reaction was to ask, "who the hell negotiated this thing?"[39] After thirty-five years of quiet obscurity, the ANWFZ Treaty was a somewhat ironic catalyst to force the administration to confront the tensions in its own nuclear policies. As a microcosm of the divisions in the administration, however, the deliberations over whether to sign are revealing.

From the outset, there were two distinct policy frameworks, which were bound to collide. From a political standpoint, it was assumed that the United States would sign the protocol with enthusiasm, a view shared by the State Department, Arms Control and Disarmament Agency (ACDA), and at least initially, the White House. In general, the United States was a supporter of nuclear-free zones and was a signatory to similar agreements for Latin America and the South Pacific.[40] The prospect of using nuclear weapons in Africa was so implausible that it barely warranted consideration. President Mandela's support for the U.S. po-

77

sition in the Nuclear Non-Proliferation Treaty was critical in persuading states to agree to its extension. Vice President Albert Gore, moreover, was planning a trip to South Africa in April 1996 and wanted to announce U.S. signature of the protocol during his visit. For Pentagon officials, by contrast, the prospect of signing a binding agreement to forswear the use of—or the threats to use—nuclear weapons was unwise for several reasons. U.S. policy regarding negative security assurances had never been seen in the Defense Department as legally binding. It was considered vitally important to protect the status of this pledge as "just a policy." As a practical matter, the Defense Department believed that the United States had always had the right to preempt or respond with nuclear weapons in a crisis, a requirement that had grown in perceived importance in light of the spread of chemical and biological weapons and of nuclear facilities being built in Iraq, Libya, and North Korea.

The timing perhaps could not have been worse. Secretary of Defense William Perry had in March issued a series of public warnings to Libya— a party to the ANWFZ Treaty—to stop construction of an alleged underground chemical facility in Tarhunah, forty miles from Tripoli. The United States intended to prevent its completion, Perry stated in congressional testimony, and "is fully prepared to take more drastic, preventative measures to accomplish this."[41] In the context of the broader discussion—that the United States would consider nuclear responses to chemical attacks—Perry's statements were interpreted as a considered policy decision, a commitment to reserve the right to launch preemptive nuclear strikes as part of the administration's counterproliferation strategy. It was also consistent with remarks Perry had made in congressional hearings. In a hearing before the Senate Armed Services Committee on March 28, 1996, Secretary Perry, trying to elicit the support of senators for the Chemical Weapons Convention, assured them that the United States has adequate capabilities to deter chemical weapons attacks without resort to U.S. chemical forces: "We have an effective range of alternative capabilities to deter or retaliate against use of the CW [chemical weapons]. The whole range would be considered. . . . We have conventional weapons, also advanced chemical weapons— precision-guided munitions, tomahawk land-attack missiles—and then we have nuclear weapons."[42]

Pentagon concerns over adherence to the ANWFZ Treaty were not limited to events in Libya, however. Whereas other nuclear-free zone agreements had not involved countries with arsenals containing weapons of mass destruction, there was "a trend here," according to a Pentagon critic, with the United States progressively forswearing its nuclear prerogative without adequate concern for the growing restrictions being placed on U.S. strategy.[43] It was, in some minds, the proverbial slippery slope.[44] In a flurry of ensuing acrimonious interagency discussions, lines were drawn around fundamentally contradictory views about nuclear weapons and U.S. interests in the third world. Individuals at the State Department, the ACDA, and the National Security Council argued that the political costs of spurning African countries and backtracking from pledges made at the Nuclear Non-Proliferation Treaty conference far outweighed the demand for nuclear options in Africa. The notion that the United States had no recourse to deter an attack by Libya or to retaliate against Libya without nuclear weapons was not compelling, and there were discussions about the ecological and radiological effects of nuclear strikes on Europe and the Middle East, to say nothing of the political effects on Russia, or even on Japan, of adopting a formal policy of nuclear use against nonnuclear states. The ACDA and some individuals at the State Department argued for signing the treaty without revision as a way to strengthen the trend toward nuclear-free zones internationally. They also sought to foreclose preemptive options in U.S. strategy, allowing that the agreement could be suspended in any case, if security were seriously imperiled.

But individuals at the Pentagon flatly opposed the U.S. signature of protocol 1 without a formal reservation protecting the U.S. right to use nuclear weapons in response to "any grave threat to U.S. security," as one participant put it.[45] The ACDA position of signing with the implicit right to violate if necessary was "irresponsible," according to a critic in the Office of the Secretary of Defense, despite the common view that such obligations are not binding in wartime.[46] One senior defense official even invoked the need to protect the sanctity of the NATO doctrine of "flexible response" and the threat to the cohesion of the alliance as a compelling reason not to sign.[47] Similarly, others raised the specter of the U.S. Navy losing access to vital facilities and its ability to navigate freely because the long-standing U.S. policy to "neither confirm nor deny" that naval platforms carry nuclear weapons would be compromised.[48] The fact that nuclear weapons had been removed from the vast majority of U.S. naval vessels was not sufficient reason to allow diplomatic arrangements to impinge on this fundamental prerogative, even if it was for all practical purposes no longer central to U.S. nuclear strategy. The Pentagon's demand threw the bureaucracy into a quandary, either to "sign a treaty but with constraints that made the agreement a joke," according to one description, or "to be forced to ask the Senate to ratify a Treaty which was opposed by the JCS," the latter option being considered particularly sensitive in a presidential election year.[49] The invocation of opposition by the Joint Chiefs of Staff came from a Pentagon civilian, however, not from active pressure from the chiefs. Confined to a small number of midlevel officials, the ensuing interagency discussions focused on finding a way to finesse this fundamental contradiction.

Based on months of tortured efforts to find a legal basis for compromise, the bureaucracy produced a "split the difference" resolution, which would allow the United States to sign the ANWFZ Treaty without a formal reservation but without forswearing nuclear prerogatives. At a White House press briefing on the day the United States signed the agreement, Robert Bell stated that "under Protocol I, which we signed, each party pledges not to use or threaten to use nuclear weapons against an ANFZ [sic] party. However, Protocol I will not limit options available to the United States in response to an attack by an ANFZ party using weapons of mass destruction."[50] The exception was based on the invocation of a little-known rule of international customary law known as "belligerent reprisals," which allows states to retaliate against illegal acts by adversaries in wartime.[51]

For Robert Bell and others, this was an optimal outcome under the circumstances, crafted deliberately to allow the competing factions to declare victory. The United States can legally suspend its obligations under the treaty in the event of aggression with chemical or biological weapons, but only in a "proportionate, limited way" aimed at a specific threat. It tempers the rationale for U.S. nuclear preemption, according to this logic: "This is not Curtis Lemay or Rolling Thunder," a National Security Council official argues, but a way to reinforce U.S. deterrence without jettisoning critical political interests.[52] The likelihood of a U.S. president ordering nuclear strikes against Africa is so remote that it tests credulity, but the policy of belligerent reprisal ensures that enemies will never be sure. Perhaps most important, "belligerent reprisal" was seen as crucial to a domestic political strategy needed to assure the Senate that in signing the protocol the United States was not foreclosing any military options. As a practical matter, variations of "belligerent reprisal" are long-standing assumptions in nuclear plans. It has long been assumed in the Pentagon that diplomatic constraints would be rendered meaningless in a time of crisis, a view taken so much for granted that it came as a surprise to some of the non-Pentagon participants.

In the final analysis, the deliberations over the ANWFZ Treaty brought the unresolved issues of targeting nonnuclear states, postponed in the nuclear posture review, to a head—but without concrete resolution or genuine consensus. In the effort to defuse potentially damaging controversy in an election year, civilian officials created the accepted declaratory rationale for what had come to be de facto military missions. This policy revision formalized notions of nuclear options for nonnuclear threats, albeit in a modulated and more politically acceptable way than might have been the case if Pentagon insistence to add a treaty reservation had prevailed. In the end, the decision reinforced "ambiguity" as the key rationale of U.S. nuclear doctrine. Secretary of Defense William Perry reiterated this policy on several occasions, stating in congressional testimony about the chemical weapons convention, for example, that the United States would rely on both conventional and nuclear weapons to respond to chemical aggression, and that "the response will be absolutely overwhelming and devastating."[53]

Confusion over U.S. policy persists within the administration. At a press briefing a few weeks after the announcement, for example, Harold Smith, assistant to the secretary of defense for atomic energy, stated explicitly that the United States lacked the conventional capability to destroy the Libyan chemical facility and would require a nuclear option until such a capability is developed. He stressed the importance of the newly accelerated program to develop the B-61-11 warhead, a "modification" of the 1960s-vintage B-53 earth-penetrating gravity bomb, which can apparently destroy underground structures with greater efficiency and much reduced collateral damage. Pentagon spokesman Kevin Bacon attempted in early May 1996 to correct the impression left by Smith that the United States had accepted a policy of nuclear preemption against Libya, stressing that if military options were necessary to counter the Libyan chemical facility, "we can accomplish this with conventional means."[54]

Conflicting statements aside, the heightened perception of threats emerging from countries that have resorted to deeply buried underground facilities to hide clandestine weapons programs have prompted active consideration of weapons concepts and doctrines useful for third world challenges. The effort by the Pentagon and the Department of Energy to portray the B-61-11 as a modification, not a new capability, is complicated. Despite protracted bureaucratic efforts to the contrary, military analysts either criticize or hail this development as a move toward low-yield nuclear options for use in regional contingencies.[55] The enduring challenge of earth penetrators is to develop sufficient accuracy and precision to destroy targets without massive collateral damage, avoiding the risks to the user and to noncombatants, which has longed plagued the effective military application of nuclear arsenals.

Some officials and private experts began in 1996 to urge that the United States update its declaratory policy and to state that the United States would never initiate the use of weapons of mass destruction against a potential aggressor.[56] This variation on classical nuclear first-use doctrine is of course misleading, since the United States does not have a chemical or biological force, but it is somehow thought by some to be an advantageous political compromise that obscures opposing notions of nuclear deterrence. The notion is that states who believe that U.S. pledges in the Nuclear Non-Proliferation Treaty not to target non-nuclear countries are binding would find this artifice somehow reassuring. Whatever their perceived military merits, similarly, consideration of nuclear designs tailored for regional application calls into question the meaning of commitments that the United States accepted when it signed the Comprehensive Test Ban Treaty, an agreement described by the administration's chief arms control official as precluding "new 'mininuke' and 'micronuke' concepts—technologies designed to use nuclear explosive yields in small amounts." The whole purpose of the Comprehensive Test Ban Treaty, as this official stated in Geneva in l996 in trying to persuade states to sign, is "to end development of advanced new weapons and keep new military applications from emerging."[57]

U.S.commitment to the Comprehensive Test Ban Treaty, however, was closely associated with the initiation of a $40 billion, ten-year program to maintain nuclear research, development, and production capability under the stockpile stewardship and management program (SSMP). In this case, there is little evidence to support the assertion that U.S. conduct represents a radical break with cold war policies. President Clinton followed on President Bush's 1991 announcement that the United States would no longer develop nuclear weapons by promising to pursue the Comprehensive Test Ban Treaty. At the same time, the Clinton administration has repeatedly reaffirmed the United States' right to withdraw from such obligations as well as to preserve the ability to maintain modern nuclear forces without testing: "In the event that I were informed by the Secretary of Defense and Secretary of Energy—advised by the Nuclear Weapons Council, the Directors of DOE's nuclear weapons laboratories and commander of U.S. Strategic Command—that a high level of confidence in the safety or reliability of a nuclear weapons type, which the two Secretaries consider to be critical to our nuclear deterrent, could no longer be certified, I would be prepared, in consultation with Congress, to exercise our 'supreme national interests' rights under the CTBT [Comprehensive Test Ban Treaty] in order to conduct whatever testing might be required."[58]

The drift toward policies for regional nuclear deterrence may test further the resilience of decisions not to develop new concepts and designs for nuclear weapons. Deterrence has never been a static concept or one that can be based on "the existential threat." It is a safe bet that an accepted regional deterrent strategy will require a commensurate architecture of operations, including more robust plans for targeting and execution, in order to be "compelling." As two analysts from Los Alamos Nuclear Laboratory argue, "We doubt that any president would authorize the use of the nuclear weapons in our present arsenal against Third World nations. It is precisely this doubt that leads us to argue for the development of subkiloton weapons."[59] Without the demonstration of "usability"—in this case, by developing weapons "whose power is effective but not abhorrent"—a tyrant could otherwise be emboldened by the belief that United States, with its "emphasis on proportionality," would be reluctant to act.

These arguments could have been lifted from the debates of the 1960s, when massive retaliation was seen as lacking in credibility precisely for the reasons cited by the Los Alamos scientists—and leading in turn to refinements in doctrine, from flexible response in the 1960s to Presidential Decision Directive 59 and credible counterforce in the 1970s and early 1980s to the innovations for protracted nuclear engagements of the 1980s. The logic of self-deterrence advanced by Aspin and others, suggesting that the United States might be paralyzed by a handful of rogue weapons because it lacked the means to deter them successfully, helped to reincarnate the core rationales for flexible targeting and operations, not just against a formidable nuclear adversary but now against states that may not even have nuclear weapons.

Current U.S. policy does not endorse the development of forces for use in regional contingencies. The doctrine of belligerent reprisal—or however operational doctrine is described—may legitimate demands for the deployment of forces designed for small-scale and preemptive attacks. But it does not necessarily imply a greater willingness on the part of the United States to use nuclear weapons. According to officials, quite the contrary: "The whole point is to enhance deterrence. No one believes we would ever attack Libya—we just want them to think we would."[60]

CHAPTER FIVE

Conclusions and Recommendations

THE CLINTON ADMINISTRATION'S EFFORTS to adapt nuclear strategy after the cold war do not yet amount to a strategic framework to guide decisions about the role and utility of nuclear forces. Much as the administration's relationship with Russia remains ambiguous—not adversarial, yet not strictly cordial—the administration's nuclear policies suffer from similar tensions and ambiguities. The administration has won notable achievements in its arms control and nonproliferation objectives, including denuclearizing the former Soviet republics, winning majority support for the Nuclear Non-Proliferation Treaty, and averting a catastrophic showdown over nuclear developments in North Korea. But it has also demonstrated an inability to advance cooperative ventures with Russia—not least to conclude and move beyond START II, which was signed by President Bush—or to articulate nonproliferation objectives clearly. Whether the security assurances granted as part of the Nuclear Non-Proliferation Treaty are legally binding or are simply political pledges that would be ignored in a crisis, for example, remains unresolved.

This situation is not unique to nuclear issues. Facing the challenge of articulating U.S. defense policy in a radically changed post–cold war environment, the Clinton administration conducted no fewer than four major reviews of U.S. national security policy. In addition to the Nuclear Posture Review (NPR), these included the 1993 Bottom-Up Review, the

1995 commission to analyze the roles and missions of the U.S. military, and the 1997 Quadrennial Defense Review. In each of these cases, senior leaders, beginning with the president, proved reluctant to engage the issues directly or to provide leadership to guide the outcome of these deliberations. As was the case with the nuclear posture review, none of these reviews proved decisive in setting clear guidelines or in forging a consensus for policy objectives.

The Bottom-Up Review did address nuclear issues in a brief section but, as mentioned earlier, deferred this issue to the upcoming Nuclear Posture Review. The preliminary conclusions of the Bottom-Up Review, however, are almost identical to the subsequent conclusions of the NPR, with the exception of minor modifications in the numbers of Trident submarines and Minuteman missiles said to be required. "Two principal guidelines shape our future requirements for strategic nuclear forces," the Bottom-Up Review stated in October 1993, "providing an effective deterrent while remaining within START I and II limits, and allowing for additional forces to be reconstituted in the event of a threatening reversal of events." This is the essential logic of lead and hedge, a strategy that emerged after a ten-month struggle to evaluate the premises and objectives of the U.S. nuclear posture.[1]

As the case studies indicate, current U.S. nuclear weapons policy may have as much to do with papering over domestic policy differences as with securing U.S. interests against potential aggression. Agreed-on guidelines for future nuclear policy continue to elude consensus, even within the government, to say nothing of the Congress and private experts. When asked for a definition of current nuclear doctrine, most officials respond that it is still deterrence, but few agree as to what deterrence means for the size, mission, or utility of the arsenal. As nuclear issues recede from public attention, the guidelines for the employment of nuclear weapons that have evolved over the last few years raise little doubt about the deepening reluctance to reduce reliance on nuclear weapons now, nearly ten years after the collapse of the Berlin Wall.

At a time when the potential for U.S. leadership seems to be great, and when the international system is in a state of relative stability, the hesitation to chart a clearer course cannot be explained fully by the risks of external uncertainty. As in other areas of foreign policy, the pressure of domestic adaptation to an uncertain world has combined with the leadership style of the president to discourage a long-term strategy in favor of tactics and compromise. A Russian commentator notes that "contradictory impulses and actions reflect [the Clinton] administration's lack of overall strategic guidelines. They leave the strong impression that Clinton's foreign policy is determined by immediate reactions to internal and, to a lesser degree, external factors."[2]

The decisions that emerged from the 1993–94 Nuclear Posture Review and that accompanied the signing of the protocol for the Africa Nuclear Weapons–Free Zone (ANWFZ) Treaty in 1996 reinforced the operational and political importance of nuclear weapons. Taken together, these decisions ratified a triad of nuclear forces, with diminished but still large numbers of strategic forces; renewed the U.S. commitment to initiate the use of nuclear weapons against existing and potential new adversaries; and granted political approval for targeting plans to develop nuclear options against regional and nonnuclear contingencies. Threats of calculated Soviet strategic attack on the United States or of an invasion of Western Europe have been replaced by scenarios in which Russia reverts to authoritarian rule and revives hostility to the West; China emerges as a determined nuclear adversary; or a third world government sponsors nuclear terrorism.[3]

An Assessment of Current Policies

For critics of the administration's renewed emphasis on robust deterrence, there are four primary reasons this policy may prove more problematic than advantageous. First, the size and organization of the nuclear force posture in the United States and Russia present risks of inadvertent or accidental execution and, as important, send powerful signals to allies and adversaries about the importance of nuclear operations, which may not be consonant with stated objectives to seek reductions in nuclear arsenals. Second, the posture is expensive to maintain and diverts resources from more pressing security challenges, including improvements in conventional forces and defenses against more likely scenarios of limited nuclear or other nonconventional strikes. Third, the retention of elaborate targeting plans against Russia, especially targeting categories such as leadership and infrastructure, are simply out of sync with the realities of modern Russia, whose economy and society are so weakened that internal collapse and political chaos, not calculated aggression, should be a far more urgent concern. Finally, there is serious concern that nuclear threats against fledgling or nonnuclear powers not only lack credibility but also impose political costs, reaffirming the importance of nuclear-based security and contradicting the objectives, which the United States fought for at the Nuclear Non-Proliferation Treaty conference.

The spectrum of competing views in the expert community and the Congress about the nuclear force posture is extremely wide. Alternatives include the elimination of nuclear weapons, a posture of minimum deterrence (with 200 weapons or fewer), proposals for developing low-yield weapons for intervention in third world conflicts, and encouraging allies and friends to acquire nuclear weapons through a system of "managed proliferation."[4] The two main areas of contention within this debate, however, focus first on the priority accorded to nuclear safety and the need to reduce the risks of unauthorized nuclear attack relative to nuclear deterrence and second on the role of military countermeasures, including nuclear operations, to manage and constrain the risks of the global diffusion of technology.

Strategic Forces

By early 1998, international events conspired with the more hard-line predilections in the Congress to deepen skepticism about the future of the U.S.-Russian partnership. What had seemed to some to be promising reasons to move to a posture of mutual assured safety, as Defense Secretary William Perry called it, were encountering more pronounced domestic political obstacles. The uncertainty of conditions in Russia is a double-edged sword. Far from prompting further force reductions or changes in U.S. force plans, the potential for instability in Russia has fueled fears of a resurgent Russian adversary, arguing for greater, not less, nuclear vigilance.

As of mid-1998, the START process remained hostage to the volatility of the two sides' domestic politics and the resulting intensification of suspicion about the other's motivations and objectives, including disputes about ballistic missile defenses and NATO enlargement. The disagreements over START II force reductions and related measures are symptoms of the current uncertainty in U.S.-Russian relations. Domestic politics in each country are in collision with efforts to advance the U.S.-Russian partnership, and common objectives sought by the two governments are fraught with domestically imposed constraints. In the United States, growing skepticism about Russian intentions have forced the Clinton administration to dedicate excessive attention to defusing critics of arms control in ways that inevitably compete with and help to curtail the scope of U.S.-Russian cooperation.

In what was to be a harbinger of this growing congressional criticism, the Senate ratified START II in 1996 without amendment but did attach "conditions," requirements to be acted upon before ratification, as well as "declarations," which are nonbinding but are considered as serious constraints on the executive branch. The most important declaration is the stipulation, discussed earlier, that the United States should not reduce its forces below START I levels absent Russian ratification of START II and that reductions under START II should be "symmetrical." The declaration states: "It is the sense of the Senate that, in conducting the reductions mandated by the START or START II Treaty, the President should, within the parameters of the elimination schedules provided for in the START treaties, regulate reductions in the United States strategic nuclear forces so that the number of accountable warheads under the START and START II Treaties possessed by the Russian Federation in no case exceeds the comparable number of accountable warheads possessed by the United States to an extent that a strategic imbalance endangering the national security interests of the United States results."[5] The proposals that emerged from the March 1997 Clinton-Yeltsin summit to consider START III and to give Russia more time to comply with existing agreements have already been criticized in the Congress and may prove controversial if brought to the Senate for ratification. Senator Strom Thurmond (R-S.C.), chairman of the Senate Armed Services Committee, said in March 1997 that he was "deeply concerned" about U.S. proposals to Russia in the Helsinki summit for further reductions in strategic nuclear weapons beyond those agreed to in START II.[6]

According to critics in the Russian Duma, the combination of an expanded NATO and existing instabilities in countries contiguous to Russia exacerbates the weaknesses of Russian conventional forces and thus make nuclear weapons more important. Officials in Moscow have stated that President Yeltsin has approved a new first-use doctrine, allowing for initiation of nuclear attacks against conventional threats, reversing a pledge by former Soviet president Mikhail Gorbachev and long-standing Soviet declaratory policy that Russian doctrine precluded using nuclear weapons against nonnuclear states. The degree to which this publicized shift in policy is politically motivated is not clear. A Russian policy of nuclear first use corresponds to a NATO doctrine of decades' duration, and NATO has long resisted political pressure to renounce this posture, including that from Russia.[7] Although the United States pledged in May 1997 not to station nuclear forces on the territories of new NATO members as part of the NATO Russia Founding Act, weaknesses in Russia's conventional forces and its perceived vulnerability to surprise attack, including by U.S. and British Trident submarine-launched ballistic missiles (SLBMs), overshadow political reassurances extended by the United States. And U.S. development of theater missile defenses as well as a renewed emphasis on nationwide defenses have reinforced Russian suspicions that the United States is still seeking technological superiority at Russia's expense.[8]

Even if START II were to be implemented in the near term, moreover, there is little indication that political and military objectives would be better harmonized at these lower force levels. Under START II, the United States and Russia would each have 3,500 deployed strategic warheads, but the agreement imposes no limits on nondeployed warheads or tactical nuclear weapons. Under the hedge strategy, the United States plans to retain 5,000 additional strategic warheads, which could be used for rapid upload. Added to the nonstrategic arsenals, this means that the actual number of weapons held by each side would be closer to 10,000 than 3,500. Both sides also would maintain the technical capability to launch thousands of nuclear weapons within minutes of warning. In the United States, all land-based missiles and the majority of submarine-based missiles would still operate on high alert. The possibility for rapid breakout is apparent on both sides but has proven particularly problematic among Russian critics of START II, who believe the United States has overwhelming technical and numerical advantages.[9]

On the U.S. side, support for lower force numbers under START III may depend upon the maintenance of the essential structure, capabilities, and doctrine of the existing posture, including how the forces would be "used in wartime." General Eugene Habiger, STRATCOM commander, stipulated in 1997 that the United States should not make a unilateral decision to reduce land-based missiles below the 500 allowed under START II, an agreement that would require an "absolutely foolproof" verification system for reductions in Russian land-based missiles, which was likely to be extremely difficult given that most Russian missiles are mobile.[10]

With Russia's numerically large nuclear arsenal and weakening command and control, the threat of accidental or unauthorized attack continues to grow, as does a flourishing clandestine trade in proscribed technologies through private ventures or crime syndicates. The weakened control of nuclear assets could result in sudden and massive proliferation. Concerns about the security and control of the arsenal under conditions of political upheaval, the challenges of safe disposition of excess nuclear materials, and the potential diffusion of nuclear assets to other countries should accordingly transcend the central objective of ensuring a robust deterrent with smaller forces. Continued reliance on forces capable of prompt strategic interaction not only impedes progress toward denuclearization but also leaves the threat of inadvertent escalation in the event of crisis.[11]

The objectives of deterring Russia and the need to address new nuclear dangers are not necessarily a zero-sum game: deterrence, it is widely agreed, is still vital as long as opposing nuclear forces exist. But in the context of stalled progress toward stabilizing reductions in Russian forces, the pointed emphasis on robust deterrence is counterproductive. Among many commentators who share this view, Fred Ikle, undersecretary of defense for policy in the Reagan administration, stresses that large numbers of nuclear weapons and plans for their use perpetuate tensions in the U.S.-Russian relationship and impose a cold war calculus on each side's military establishment: "Military staffs on each side will continue to perform calculations to estimate whether the Other Side (who used to be the enemy) could somehow launch a first strike without having to fear massive and certain retaliation." For Ikle, maintaining activated forces stems from "Cold War imagery, [which] is likely to persist, like a genetic defect, well after the conflict itself has ended."[12]

A leaked Central Intelligence Agency study in March 1997 reported several examples of the deterioration of the Russian nuclear infrastructure and the growing risks of the loss of controls over weapons.[13] The stressed condition of Russia's command and control system means that the potential for forces to be launched in response to false warning needs to be taken seriously. In such a scenario, Russia faces the risk of U.S. retaliation to what was in reality an accidental strike. Reports that Russian nuclear forces were activated and well into preparations for nuclear strikes in January 1995 in response to a false signal of a U.S. SLBM attack—a Norwegian scientific rocket was confirmed by Russian military officers to be a U.S. missile on a trajectory toward Moscow—provides one example of the potential dangers of reliance on forces that must be launched promptly. The CIA report summarized it: "Fearing system decapitation, Soviet and Russian military leaders traditionally have been more concerned with maintaining a robust launch capability over negative control to exclude accidental or unauthorized launch."[14]

The fragility of Russian society suggests that the United States should be moving more aggressively to induce Russia to reduce its arsenal before it is too late, an objective better served by agreements to shrink stockpiles and to take weapons off alert than by a hedge strategy. A report of a Council on Foreign Relations task force on nuclear proliferation, chaired by Stephen Hadley, emphasized: "In addition to implementing agreed reductions, the United States should take steps . . . to 'lengthen the nuclear fuse' by: lowering alert rates on strategic nuclear forces; deactivating, disabling and disassembling nuclear delivery systems destined for reduction and elimination; and 'escrowing' nuclear weapons removed from those systems."[15] Fred Ikle argues that the continued reliance on prompt nuclear operations is an atavism of the 1960s:

> The NATO policy of flexible response, which threatens first use of nuclear weapons, did more harm than good by encouraging both the U.S. and Russia to adopt highly dangerous "hair trigger" alert postures. Russia's reliance on a "hair trigger" posture constitutes the clearest nuclear threat to U.S. security. Reductions of forces can do quite a bit of good, but we must consider what happens with the remaining forces. . . . The U.S. and Russian militaries should launch a joint program to reduce the readiness of their nuclear forces. The agreed procedures might include separating warheads from missiles, partially dismantling missiles, or other steps that could be monitored and could be implemented rapidly and without waiting for scheduled START reductions.[16]

There is no agreement within the U.S. government as to whether further steps in reducing alert levels are feasible, how these steps would be implemented, or whether they would support U.S.-Russian nuclear stability. In addition, no new initiatives to change operational practices have been advanced pending ratification of START II by the Russian

Duma. The need to reduce the alert status of land- and submarine-based weapons tends to be dismissed by many officials as militarily unsound and, in any case, unnecessary, for several reasons. For many, the risks of accidental launch seem exaggerated. There are elaborate procedures in place, they argue, to prevent U.S. leaders from making decisions based on faulty or falsified information, and fail-safe measures are in place to control crisis response and unwarranted escalation. The Russian command and control system, though monitored carefully by U.S. intelligence for new developments, is basically reliable, and risks of accidental exchange are thus quite low.

Those involved in force planning also dispute the idea that removing warheads from deployed weapons would increase stability by providing more time for nuclear preparations, in case of a crisis. Such a scheme, according to this view, could actually increase the vulnerability of forces by compounding the risks of sudden breakout and inviting adversaries to attack. De-alerting schemes are predicated on strict standards of verification and transparency, but critics insist that a surprise attack scenario is made more likely with de-alerted forces, since an enemy could cheat and then be able to assume that no credible retaliation would follow. A Council on Foreign Relations study chaired by Larry Welch, air force chief of staff, concluded that "the rationale for additional de-posturing would be primarily to give more warning of preparations for possible intentional use or perhaps more extended cooling-off period in crisis. . . . The question is how to ensure that regeneration capability, retained for orderly adjustments in the event of worsening political conditions or the possible deterioration of some part of the nuclear forces, would not provide the basis for a rapid and destabilizing break-out."[17] Despite overwhelming superiority, the United States might even lose the ability to offset the conventional capabilities of current and future adversaries who wield a nuclear capability.[18] The fundamental basis for disagreement between proponents and opponents of constraints on operational readiness hinge in large measure on the degree to which each believes that the risk of deliberate rather than inadvertent U.S.-Russian nuclear aggression remains high. For those who believe Russia is and will remain an aggressor, calculations of force parity and other cold war counting measures remain crucial, as does the ability to reverse arms control achievements quickly (by uploading or regenerating forces) in crisis.

The current stalemate in reducing and redirecting the Russian strategic force posture is an expensive and potentially dangerous legacy of the Clinton administration's failure to advance the START process, a stalemate that has to be addressed with greater urgency. Current uncertainties in both sides' domestic politics aside, the United States and Russia need a far more comprehensive road map to articulate common objectives than currently is possible with a fixation on negotiated force reductions. As a first step, the United States should seek to open a strategic dialogue with the Russians—not a discussion of the next steps in START but rather a wide-ranging exploration of the two sides' overall objectives, plans, and postures as the two sides move into a new strategic relationship. Over time, the two sides should seek to open more specific talks on means to maintain a stable U.S.-Russian partnership as part of a move to smaller and safer nuclear forces, including, inter alia, harmonization of strategic doctrines and of policies guiding the alert status of forces, joint warning, and the potential contribution of defenses in building mutual confidence as force levels decline.

At a minimum, these talks should accelerate efforts begun in 1992 to cooperate in early-warning technology and systems, a subject taken up at the May 1998 Clinton-Yeltsin summit. An agreement reached after the summit will allow for the two sides to share data about missile and space launches, a potentially critical measure when Russian early-warning systems face continued and increasingly risky degradation.[19] If brought to fruition, this initial step could result in the establishment of a joint American-Russian command center, potentially providing a means for the two sides to communicate about strategic missile warnings and, perhaps, about developing country missile programs as well.

As the ratification of START II by the Duma has become increasingly enmeshed in intensifying internal political struggles, budget crises, and hard-line opposition to various U.S. policies, the "treaty of hope," as Boris Yeltsin described it to George Bush in 1993, has become an albatross to the U.S.-Russian relationship. Russian nuclear forces seem almost certain to fall well below START II levels within the next ten years. Their age and condition, and the limited resources available for replacements, make this almost inevitable. START II has acquired a symbolic and political importance well beyond its concrete benefits. The insistence by the administration and the Congress of the need to have Russia ratify this agreement before new initiatives can be considered is causing the U.S. government to spend funds it does not want to spend on forces the U.S. military does not want to acquire. On the Russian side, the Duma's symbolic need to oppose one critical U.S. (and Yeltsin) demand is causing friction, which could lead to the unraveling of the whole foundation for cooperation. Without abandoning the process entirely—agreements are needed to ensure that force structures, not just force levels, are adjusted in a mutually advantageous way—the United States should more aggressively propose measures to alleviate Russian concerns. At this point, a system of reciprocal, unilateral reductions backed up by inspections and other confidence-building measures could give each side more political latitude to accomplish what it wants to do anyway. A quiet discussion of this kind could help build a process of reciprocity that achieves common goals.[20]

That said, the administration or its successor needs to lead the American people in a more active discussion of the strategic posture and of the emerging nuclear dangers. The Congress and the specialist community in and out of government have been engaging in stale debates for so long that all sides have forgotten the public's lack of comprehension. Within the elite debate, the absence of leadership helps perpetuate out-of-date, arcane positions that are argued in a manner to elude constructive consensus. With key elements of the policy community behind it—not least the Joint Chiefs of Staff—the administraton has the opportunity to build a new consensus on strategic policy. This consensus in the near term should embrace the benefits to American security of continuing to reduce offensive weapons and of improving the security and safety of Russian forces.

Cooperative Ventures

Russian delays in ratifying START II also have encouraged growing domestic political opposition to funding for cooperative threat reduction. The success of Senators Sam Nunn (D-Ga.) and Richard Lugar (R-Ind.) in winning support for Department of Defense appropriations to assist the states of the former Soviet Union in weapon dismantlement and security appears to have been a transitory moment of bipartisanship and congressional reason. Passed in 1991, the Nunn-Lugar cooperative threat reduction program provided $400 million annually between fiscal year 1992 and fiscal year 1993, with additional increments ranging from $300 million to $400 million between 1994 and fiscal year

1996. By the time of the fiscal year 1996 budget request, this included an additional $371 million for ongoing projects, which the House Committee on National Security cut to $200 million. In fiscal year 1999, the administration requested $442.2 million; the House cut this amount to $417.4, but the Senate restored it to the original amount, and this level prevailed.[21]

The hindrances to cooperation posed by Russian politics and by faulty implementation of initiatives cannot be exaggerated. Given the paramount importance to U.S. security of nuclear safety in Russia, however, U.S. efforts to overcome impediments posed by the Russians have not been a high enough priority at senior levels. According to a bipartisan task force sponsored by the Council on Foreign Relations and the Nixon Center for Peace and Freedom, "Washington's response to the new threat of nuclear leakage [from Russia] has not equaled U.S. stakes in the matter."[22] Additional constraints placed by Congress include stipulations that Nunn-Lugar funds go to American contractors under a "buy American" mandate and that funds not be used to assist Russian domestic priorities, such as housing for unemployed military officers. Although these provisions reflect congressional concerns that Russia would divert funds to domestic needs in order to preserve scarce capital for military priorities, the result has been a lack of compelling inducements for Russia to accept cooperative denuclearization as a central priority.

It is an anomaly of U.S. politics that a majority of members of Congress perceive the Nunn-Lugar agenda as foreign aid and, as such, seek to slash, if not eliminate, its modest funding. As one extreme example, analysts from the Heritage Foundation urged the Senate in 1995 to cancel funding for Nunn-Lugar to allow funds for additional B-2 bombers, preferring to spend billions to add a few deliverable weapons rather than to eliminate an exponentially higher number of weapons from the Russian inventory that could be targeted against the United States. In a country that bears the burden of a $270 billion defense budget with a minimum of controversy (except perhaps to increase spending, as called for in the defense authorization bills of fiscal years 1996 and 1997), the tiny fraction of funds allocated for dismantling and imposing controls over the former Soviet arsenal is dismissed by critics as ill advised or as competitive with more urgent priorities.[23]

Despite considerable success by midlevel officials in initiating projects throughout the former Soviet Union—an achievement that required gaining the confidence of new and former adversarial governments and carefully demonstrating the credibility of the U.S. commitment to these states' security—such projects have never been granted the importance they deserved, perhaps in part because they were never publicized effectively by the administration.[24] There was never a concerted White House effort to sell the program to the Congress. Since the departure of Secretary of Defense William Perry, whose testimony and public statements consistently and eloquently emphasized the criticality of this agenda despite mounting political opposition, there has been no clear champion in the administration to promote these initiatives. The failure to integrate cooperative threat reduction programs into the core of U.S. security planning and to elicit enduring public support for these objectives may prove to be one of the most serious opportunity costs of domestic politics on U.S. policy.

Deterring Rogue States

The extension of the Nuclear Non-Proliferation Treaty, widely considered a triumph for U.S. leadership, was treated in its aftermath as a "vote count," with the goal defined as getting majority support at the review conference, not as a successful referendum on the importance and credibility of the nonnuclear regime. To the contrary, the declarations signed by the United States to gain the support of third world countries have been consigned to the background of diplomatic rhetoric and, in some circles, denied operational or legal status. As was the case during the cold war, these pledges are seen by many as needless intrusions into the latitude of the United States to define and implement its security objectives without reference to other states' agendas, as witnessed in the debates accompanying the decision to sign the ANWFZ Treaty. One result has been an as yet undefined U.S. strategy to consider the use of nuclear weapons to deter nonnuclear threats. The Clinton administration's view seems to have evolved toward a view that increases in regional nuclear (and chemical and biological) weapon development programs impose pressure on the United States to maintain and adapt nuclear operations against new threats, although the details of how the United States would implement such a policy are still in dispute. The internal divisions between U.S. declaratory policy and operational policy are still very much in evidence.

Since the early 1990s, there have been two opposing perspectives in the U.S. debate about regional nuclear operations. The first, espoused especially by State Department and UN officials, is that an emphasis on nuclear operations has no positive effect in advancing nonproliferation. Adapting targeting plans to include potential regional powers that do not have nuclear weapons is in violation of the stated policy of the United States and the promises made in 1995 as part of the bargain to extend the Nuclear Non-Proliferation Treaty. According to one legal scholar, "The 1995 presidential promise [at the NPT] clearly prohibits a pre-emptive U.S. nuclear strike [against a nonnuclear state] . . . the conse-quences of putting it aside would be catastrophic for international efforts to prevent the spread of nuclear weapons. The promise was sol-emnly made not just by the United States but by Britain, France, and Russia. China went even further to promise it would never use nuclear weapons first. . . . The promises were made to over 170 non-nuclear weapon NPT parties as part of the quid pro quo for their support for extending the NPT and making it permanent."[25] A strategy to threaten nuclear use, however indirect, may abet proliferation by promoting the perception that the nonproliferation regime exists solely for the self-serving interests of the minority nuclear powers. The only utility of nuclear weapons, in this view, is to deter other nuclear weapons.

The opposing view, captured in a study commissioned by the joint strategic target planning staff in 1991, is that the United States should "reject the thesis that the only purpose of nuclear weapons in the New World Order is to deter nuclear attack, or the threat of nuclear attack. . . . The U.S. should adopt neither a declaratory nor an employ-ment policy which suggests that American nuclear weapons are called upon only to deter other nuclear states."[26] Deepening doubts about the seriousness of diplomatic arrangements to enforce nonproliferation norms coincide with the perceived need to demonstrate instruments that the United States could use to defeat new forms of aggression. The extension of the Nuclear Non-Proliferation Treaty in 1995 was a pyrrhic victory, according to this view, papering over severe schisms in the in-ternational community about the viability of the regime while exclud-ing the key proliferant states that pose the most urgent risks to interna-tional security. Efforts by lawless states to acquire capabilities that would threaten the United States will continue regardless of the support by 186 states for the agreement's extension. For some, diplomatic arrange-ments of this kind, including the 1994 framework agreement with North

Korea and the decision to loosen sanctions against China in return for its nonproliferation pledges, represent an expensive capitulation by the United States, which are bound to fail in curtailing the trade in nuclear technologies and, further, will damage U.S. credibility.[27]

The most commonly cited scenarios in which the United States might have to use or threaten to use nuclear weapons are against states that threaten U.S. forces or territory with nuclear and biological weapons or with chemical weapons on a large scale.[28] Even advocates acknowledge that there are severe technical and operational challenges to overcome in making such a policy credible or effective. Nuclear retaliation against chemical or biological use would have to be perceived as proportionate, which would require precise targeting of military assets or troops.[29] Collateral damage and civilian casualties would have to be seriously constrained to avoid invoking normative concerns as great as or greater than those raised by the initial use of chemical or biological weapons by an adversary. Even precision targeting could result in large-scale civilian damage (especially if intelligence about installations and leadership bunkers remains uncertain, as is likely). Alternatively, a retaliatory strike could have such low yields that the attacks either will not be effective or could be carried out with conventional weapons.[30] Nuclear use in conflicts involving U.S. or allied troops, in turn, may pose risks to Americans disproportionate to the benefits. Historically, moreover, the implied threat of nuclear retaliation against states outside of the U.S.-Soviet sphere has had negligible effects on regional conflicts that impinge on or endanger U.S. interests, from Korea to Vietnam to Iraq's invasion of Kuwait.[31]

The dilemma that the United States faced in North Korea illustrates the difficulties of implementing military strikes to terminate a country's nuclear program. How could the United States, with any certainty, launch a successful preemptive strike if Pyongyang had even one nuclear warhead hidden within an underground complex? Intelligence reports were contradictory about the number of weapons North Korea had, and information about the location of nuclear devices and technologies was uncertain. It was the consensus judgment of the U.S. military and Asian allies, moreover, that any military provocation could lead to a large-scale offensive by the North in a conflict in which there could be 1 million casualties, including 80,000 to 100,000 U.S. soldiers.[32] Subsequent war games to simulate the way nuclear weapons could be used against the North reveal other operational and political constraints.

Exercises known as Nimble Dancer, conducted as part of the analysis for the Quadrennial Defense Review, contemplated tactical nuclear strikes in retaliation against North Korean chemical attacks on the South. These were judged to lack credibility because none of the participants believed that the president would authorize such a step. Consideration of conventionally armed intercontinental-range missiles strikes also were rejected because of the chance that China could misperceive these to be a nuclear attack against its territory.[33]

Israel's strike on Iraq's Osiraq nuclear reactor in 1981 stands as the textbook case of a successful preventive attack. But although most of the world may have breathed a collective sigh of relief following the Israeli operation, its longer term effects were certainly mixed. Osiraq was an object lesson not lost on states that now seek to embed clandestine military programs in hardened, underground bunkers designed to resist destruction—as North Korea, Libya, and others seem to have done. If efforts accelerate to complicate detection and destruction, such as burying facilities underground, then parallel efforts by the international community to promote strict standards of transparency, disclosure, and inspections may prove elusive. Surveillance by satellites or other technical means cannot penetrate carefully hidden facilities with the same ease that such facilities can be built. For example, a perfectly legal form of technical proliferation is occurring in machinery to dig tunnels of the kind used for the U.K.-French chunnel, acquisitions that cannot be stopped by coercive international strictures. The fallback, in such an environment, is a more abstract appeal to nuclear deterrence. But nuclear deterrence is unlikely to be compelling against terrorist threats whose origin is not clear or is diffused across national boundaries. Deterrence requires identification of the aggressor and the ability to demonstrate that its assets can be targeted effectively, an impossible task against threats from, for example, radical groups with chemical or biological devices operating clandestinely in urban environments. Deterrence in the classic sense is agreed to be largely useless in these kinds of contingency.

Given the operational constraints discussed above, faith in the ability of air strikes or in the kind of counterproliferation arrangements currently being developed to halt states' weapons programs may be misplaced. As the effort to implement UN Resolution 687—providing for the dismantlement and destruction of Iraq's arsenal—has shown, another country's military infrastructure can prove very resilient to attacks, however superior one's own forces. As the executive chairman of the UN Special Commission has repeatedly emphasized, it is the work of the inspection teams, not military strikes, that have succeeded in destroying Iraq's nonconventional arsenal—even if not altogether successfully. The core of Iraq's and other third world countries' military potential is entrenched in their industrial capabilities, their human capital, and the resources they can command to attract suppliers. How this potential is used depends on motivations. But none of these factors is readily susceptible to eradication by coercive means.

There is also the concern that excessive rhetoric about new security threats may inadvertently encourage states to acquire nuclear, chemical, or missile technologies by exaggerating the capabilities of and risks posed by rogue state arsenals. If it is true that a state with a handful of nuclear or chemical weapons can defeat Western resolve, third world countries could be expected to take this seriously, seeking the means to enhance their international status with the very instruments that the West decries. It is not useful to publicly deride U.S. and allied capabilities to respond to aggression, even if such concerns warrant attention. For critics, the linkage of nuclear deterrence and nonproliferation has marginalized policy priorities that are more urgent than targeting installations or troops. More attention needs to be given to the following: defensive programs, such as protective gear for military personnel and stepped-up intelligence against potential terrorists; the possibility of accidents or deliberate sabotage in states, such as Pakistan, with fragile nuclear infrastructures and safety precautions; the potential for enduring estrangement from some Islamic states whose attitude has grown increasingly antagonistic toward U.S. military preparations since the Gulf War; and widespread political discreditation of the international nonproliferation regime and its norms. Compared to the priority accorded to military preparations, the level of effort (and political capital) dedicated to the creation of new and more robust regimes for the international control of nuclear technologies, or more imaginative strategies for assisting states facing local and regional instability without resorting to the acquisition of weapons of mass destruction, remains highly constrained.

For now, U.S. policy is couched in political ambiguity, and the traditional split between declaratory and operational policy is preserved.

Two years after the discussion of "belligerent reprisal," administration officials are far from eager to espouse this policy publicly, and some even dispute that any such doctrine exists. In a meeting in 1997, for example, Stephen Andreas, who was Robert Bell's principal deputy on the National Security Council, was adamant that U.S. policy toward the targeting of regional powers never deviated from the 1978 Cyrus Vance policy providing for negative security assurances against non-nuclear states.[34] In February 1998, similarly, the administration, to counter a conclusion that the Yeltsin government had drawn mistakenly from administration rhetoric, issued statements that the United States had no intention of using nuclear weapons against Iraq. That said, the statement also emphasized that "we do not rule out in advance any capability available to us . . . [in a] situation in which the United States, our allies, or our forces have been attacked with chemical or biological weapons."[35] The next opportunity to discuss these issues internationally may be the next Nuclear Non-Proliferation Treaty conference in 2000, a challenge that may resemble that of 1995 but that will include further allegations from some key states that the United States is violating its security assurance pledges with new targeting plans, adaptations of nuclear weapons, and an overt refusal to abandon its policy of first use.

Deliberations that have taken place since the extension of the Nuclear Non-Proliferation Treaty in 1995 include two of four meetings of preparatory committees established to provide guidance for the conference in 2000. The issues likely to be contentious in that conference are already fairly clearly delineated, including the lack of universality in the treaty, security assurances, and nuclear weapons–free zones. Drawing on the experiences of the 1995 review conference, the administration and its successor may be able to defuse difficult controversies if enough advance attention is paid to this process. As of this writing, however, the conditions for U.S. leadership in furtherance of the treaty regime are not propitious. In addition to the absence of progress in U.S.-Russian nuclear arms reduction, the likely failure of the U.S. Senate to ratify the Comprehensive Test Ban Treaty before 2000 and confusion about the legal status of security assurances and weapons-free zone treaties can be counted on to divide the 186 members of the regime and expose the United States to protracted criticism for its apparent failiure to live up to its 1995 bargain.

Lessons Learned

The stated purpose of the Nuclear Posture Review was to conduct a thorough reevaluation of the U.S. nuclear posture, including detailed analysis of force plans and their relevance to the changing character of threats, and to provide senior leaders with options for future policy. The way it was actually conducted and its outcome may provide historians with a classic example of how not to attempt policy initiatives in sensitive areas of national security. The review process failed to challenge accepted procedures or to intrude upon the authority of a well-defined bureaucracy. In this case, the ingredients of failure included an absent president who seemed painfully intimidated by his lack of clout with the military, the loss of and failure to replace a powerful and politically astute advocate after Les Aspin's resignation as secretary of defense, political appointees operating like McNamara's Whiz Kids without memory of their predecessors' legacy, a Pentagon bureaucracy for which deflection of this initiative was hardly an effort, and a virtual absence of a domestic political strategy to help defuse predictable congressional or internal opposition. An important lesson applicable to future efforts is how politically challenging an exercise of this kind is likely to be and how impossible it is without the clout and sustained attention of senior leaders. After ten months of effort, the role and utility of nuclear weapons for managing future threats was left largely unexamined, and the status quo was essentially reaffirmed by default.

Many participants blame individuals for the limitations of the review, pointing to Aspin for underestimating the resilience of the bureaucracy to sudden changes imposed from the top, to John Deutch and William Perry for failing to back up their subordinates or to assume leadership, to Ashton Carter for his managerial inexperience, or to career bureaucrats and uniformed military officers for their ill-informed or self-interested attachment to outmoded force plans and threat perceptions. To the degree that officials should be held accountable for not conducting a genuine review and eliciting a genuine consensus, the responsible individuals are the president and his closest advisers. A vacuum in senior-level leadership and White House authority conspired with the reflexive reluctance of career professionals to accept unfamiliar concepts that tested deeply held beliefs and entrenched ways of conducting policy. Absent any clear directives originating from the president about the critical importance of adapting nuclear policies to new circumstances, the outcome was virtually guaranteed.

Based on the bureaucratic arrangements alone, it is not a mystery how the Nuclear Posture Review was transformed from a review of national policy to a force posture exercise, which, with modest exceptions, reinforced existing doctrine, targeting plans, and requirements. Participants in the review vary in their recollections of events, but they are unanimous in their conclusion that the results were practically a foregone conclusion once Aspin's connections to the president were no longer a factor. Senior officials, in turn—beginning with the White House—were quick to cave at any hint of controversy. Key officials within the Pentagon were apparently never in agreement about the objectives or even the desirability of the review. In the end, in the words of one caustic critic, the Nuclear Posture Review was "a tarbaby," handed to a politically inexperienced assistant secretary who "never even had a loyal 'point man' to carry the mandate" internally.[36] As countless episodes dating back to the 1960s demonstrate, there is a point beyond which even senior officials cannot trespass into protected territory if they are not prepared to pay the consequences.[37]

Most participants agree that Aspin and Carter did attempt to engage in deliberations over nuclear policy at a serious level, for good or ill. Questions raised by Carter and his subordinates went to the heart of the logic of cold war deterrence and its operational assumptions, challenging what had long been known to be tensions or outright contradictions in political and force planning assumptions. But Aspin's notion of a tabula rasa nuclear review never came close to reality. The analytical exercise was superficially imposed on the planning infrastructure and on career professionals who were already responding to different directives and priorities inherited from preceding administrations. Even at the height of cold war consensus, decisionmakers had never formulated or understood the importance of clear guidelines about what should be targeted, for what reason, or with what level of destructive force in a way that reflected political as well as military judgments. It was simply not a priority for leaders to expend the time and political capital needed to ensure that war plans and political goals were compatible. A small number of Clinton officials did try, at least for a time, but were not able to withstand the backlash.

Given the way in which authority is delegated for nuclear policy and planning under current arrangements, it is not accurate to attribute the outcome of the Nuclear Posture Review to simple bureaucratic inertia. The extreme political sensitivity of nuclear operations and plans to execute forces—practices sanctioned by every president since Eisenhower—require that authority for nuclear war be delegated to a decisionmaking apparatus designed specifically to discourage political intrusion. It is a system that, by its very nature, will oppose radical systemic change. The relative absence of expertise among political authorities to credibly challenge planning assumptions and to force examination of traditional premises remains the greatest weakness in crafting policies for contemporary challenges.

But perhaps the real issue is political conviction. Civilian officials traditionally have rationalized their lack of interest in nuclear force plans by stating that they doubt that the system will ever be tested. Presidents have repeatedly shown their reluctance to use nuclear weapons, and they are not likely to be swayed by pressure to do so, even in a crisis. Another reason to be unconcerned is that deterrence may be well served if adversaries draw the mistaken conclusion that the United States is intent on waging nuclear war. As long as such notions prevail, officials are unlikely to be motivated to take on the political burdens of attempting reforms of operational plans to better address current risks. Indeed, why bother? It follows that policies that do not meet with the approval of the planning community or the bureaucracy are potentially divisive. Without the benefit of informed political discourse, decisions that provoke overt opposition from professionals are bound to generate doubts in the Congress and the public about the wisdom of elected and appointed officials. Direct assaults on military authority, in particular, may provoke an immune reaction in a nation long used to deferring to their judgment in certain areas. Done carelessly, such actions are far more likely to cast doubts on those seeking innovations than to achieve any positive outcome. Even if a decision cannot be definitively shown to damage national security, any controversy sufficient to undermine the cohesion of the national command authority can be said to be against the national interest. Indeed, there is reason to believe that in the effort to avoid such conflict, it is sufficiently compelling for senior political authorities to not pursue controversial objectives.

President Clinton's stewardship of U.S. nuclear policy is unfortunately a story of missed opportunities. The president's role in directing nuclear policies has been negligible, and the debates that have occupied his subordinates apparently have remained largely unknown to him. It is not clear that the deeper implications of the conduct and outcome of the Nuclear Posture Review and the ANWFZ Treaty for presidential authority and U.S. strategy were a matter of compelling concern. If so, perhaps such concerns were dismissed as not urgent enough to fight over, given the high risk and lack of any apparent political payoff.[38] Involving the president in debates over security issues obscure to the public may simply have not been possible when the administration was already besieged by recriminations over questions such as operations in Somalia and Haiti or the debacle over the decision to allow gays to serve in the military, to say nothing of current political crises.

The Clinton legacy nevertheless stands in sharp contrast to that of his immediate predecessor.[39] Aides to President Bush are unanimous in their admiration for his leadership style, a presidential leadership that achieved a number of nuclear innovations that provoked no discernible or publicized opposition. When in 1991 President Bush ordered the Strategic Air Command to unilaterally de-alert bombers and remove launch pins from missiles, he met no appreciable resistance despite the extreme sensitivity of these measures. What accounts for Bush's success? "President Bush never let an important issue drop into the bureaucracy," one of his key advisers says; "Clinton debates objectives with his subordinates. Bush debated tactics but never objectives."[40] Bush would state his desired outcome and leave the details to subordinates, according to another description: "I want tactical nuclear weapons out of Europe. Gorbachev needs U.S. cover to get their nukes out of the republics before they collapse."[41]

Bush, in turn, could count on his main advisers to carry out his directives, individuals whose unanimity of purpose, political credibility, and bureaucratic skills could help deflect or override opposition. General Brent Scowcroft, national security adviser, General Colin Powell, chairman of the Joint Chiefs of Staff, and Secretary of Defense Richard Cheney could use their clout with the uniformed military to defuse hawkish opposition, both in the Pentagon and in the Congress. They also were astute inside players, who knew they could count on the president—and one another—in the face of opposition. President Bush, moreover, was involved in what aides call the "heavy lifting" of foreign policy, working directly and tirelessly with congressional and foreign leaders to set the stage for positive reception of U.S. initiatives. "This is simply not something that can be left to staff," said a close aide; nothing substitutes for direct presidential engagement.[42] In the end, Bush also seemed to have a far keener sense for the urgency of unfolding developments in Russia, undoubtedly assisted by his close relationship with Gorbachev. The contrast between the Bush and Clinton legacies suggests that presidential leadership can be critically important even when international realities are roughly similar.

A new policy review may be required if serious changes in the force posture are ever to be considered. Disciplining the bureaucracy to prevent sabotage is a necessary but not sufficient condition, however. Other critical considerations would determine success or failure and should inform decisions about the timing of such an undertaking. The first is the degree of genuine presidential commitment. Second is the ability of key advisers and senior officials to sustain a steady course even if opposition erupts. And third is the careful management of competing policy priorities, which may otherwise impinge on the undertaking.

Any serious review must be presidentially initiated and supervised. The president, in other words, has to stake his prestige on the success of the undertaking. Both the Bush and the Clinton experiences, as well as prior efforts at nuclear innovation, highlight the degree to which presidential authority depends on certification by senior military leaders. An interest in innovation has to compete with the risk of being deemed inexperienced, untutored, or just dangerously misguided, as happened to President Carter when he asked innocently in his first single integrated operation plan briefing why the United States needed more than "about 200" survivable missiles. Whether by compliance or overt support from professionals, maintaining credibility as commander in chief is a fragile enterprise, however popular the president may be with the public. The techniques needed to engage the establishment constructively may vary, but President Clinton, who is neither a war hero like Eisenhower nor surrounded by respected military leaders like Bush, would likely need "someone to give him footing," as a veteran of the policy wars put it. One suggestion is the appointment of a special group of senior and respected advisers to draft the charter for a presidential review, a group that would in turn provide the legitimacy and political cover needed to defuse opposition or to protect the president if there is controversy.

Bureaucracies have to be involved and, through carefully supervised participation, induced to cooperate. The most effective technique recommended by past practitioners and mastered by Henry Kissinger when he was secretary of state and national security adviser is to require agencies to develop options for high-level review, part of a process for which senior officials are made accountable. Some argue that Kissinger tasked the bureaucracy with useless work specifically to keep it occupied and unable to interfere. According to other accounts, however—including Kissinger's, as expressed in his memoirs—he was deeply involved in some of the studies and frustrated by the slow pace of other parts of the government. According to Kissinger, disciplined involvement of professionals is vital.[43] Implementing committees reporting to the senior group, in turn, could help to enforce direction and deadlines. The point is not to impose an expected outcome on the deliberations, which could be disastrous, but to put forward practical and realistic guidelines, with an implicit conception of where the agenda should come out. The objective is to elicit consensus through "concentric circles" of decisionmakers, managed from the top down.

Morton Halperin suggests a scheme for a review that would include many of these elements, including the appointment of an interagency task force, chaired by a senior Pentagon official, to conduct a study of options for the president. The task force would be assisted by personnel from each of the agencies and would consult with outside experts, including an experts group appointed by the national security adviser, who would conduct a concurrent study. The final report to the president would include current policy options, options endorsed by particular agencies, and options suggested by the experts group and private reports, each accompanied by analysis of costs and risks but without specific endorsement.[44]

As the case studies demonstrate, however, without systematic efforts to develop political-military coalitions, many of the battles ostensibly fought about defense priorities can degenerate into conflict over authority and prerogative. Not impressed that the nuclear posture review was serious, the bureaucracy and the services delegated responsibility to inexperienced subordinates and did not pay much attention until they had reason to think that political appointees were exceeding their mandates. It is not surprising that midlevel officers endorsed the status quo or that senior officers were antagonized by perceived attempts to exclude them from the decisionmaking process. The opposition to the ANWFZ Treaty, similarly, was an issue joined largely though the prism of authority and precedent, not fundamental security interests.

The bottom line for a domestic strategy is to ensure that the president be given options based on informed analysis, not bureaucratic "findings" born of low-level consensus. In the words of Martin Anderson, Reagan's domestic adviser who helped craft the strategic defense initiative while riding on Reagan's campaign plane, new initiatives have to be protected from the bureaucracy until they have some momentum, or they will "be murdered in [their] cribs."[45]

Conclusions

The debates about the U.S. nuclear posture analyzed in this study were conducted in a domestic political climate that initially seemed open to a review of assumptions and principles of nuclear security, in line with changed international circumstances. Upon closer examination, however, it became evident that policymakers were only superficially inclined to depart from long-standing premises. Opinion in the executive branch and the Congress was divided over the desirability of changes in the roles and missions assigned to nuclear forces, with a clear tilt against the political challenges posed by a devaluation of nuclear weapons of the kind implied in U.S. statements made during the Nuclear Non-Proliferation Treaty extension conference. Decisions that suggest the sanctioning of a permanently robust nuclear operation against non-nuclear threats, however, remain tentative and subject to revision. These discussions took place before the resolution of more fundamental questions, including how to interpret changes in Russia and China, the degree to which the United States wants to pursue partnership with former adversaries, and a clear definition of the utility of nuclear deterrence to dissuade the acquisition or use of weapons of mass destruction. It is possible that more active elite and public discussions about nuclear weapons could prompt a serious national (and international) debate and put pressure on this and future administrations to render current assumptions more explicit. Even more informed analysis of the premises and criteria for nuclear policies by administration officials would be significant.

For many of the senior officials interviewed for this study, including those currently serving in the Clinton administration, the content and character of nuclear plans are subordinate priorities, if they are considered at all. Whatever the size of the arsenal or the targeting strategy preferred by Pentagon planners, it is argued, the U.S. national command system is set up to ensure that the president has full authority for any contemplated use of nuclear weapons, and no president has ever shown an inclination to execute nuclear strikes. "The employment utility [of strategic weapons] had gone to zero by the late 1970s," according to a former senior military officer. Still, "the myth of their use served useful purposes. It was the backbone of alliances, even if it had no clear effect on Soviet adventurism."[46] Deterrence, however it is defined, nevertheless is valued because it helps to create ambiguity in the eyes of adversaries—a policy that serves to ensure the political status of the United States as a superpower and reliable ally. It is widely assumed that the number of nuclear weapons in the U.S. arsenal will continue to decline at least as long as Russia cooperates, and some nuclear missions will be deemphasized accordingly. Russia, not the United States, is setting the terms of the debate, and there is not much more that the United States can do unilaterally without provoking partisan opposition.

In the future, this relatively passive approach among senior policymakers may not be adequate to manage the conflicting trends in policies and U.S. opinion, especially if scenarios of nuclear use become more prominent in the public consciousness. The current arrangements, which inhibit active linkages between policymakers and defense planners, will not serve U.S. interests if nuclear weapons remain instruments of crisis diplomacy and conflict management. The uncertainties about where or when the United States would threaten to use—or actually use—nuclear forces are sufficiently high that these sites and times will elude planning by military or intelligence organizations. These centralized operations compete with procedures that take political and military dynamics more directly into account. This is not to say that policy should rely entirely on ad hoc decisionmaking, but it does suggest that decisions involving nuclear weapons must now be acknowledged to be increasingly political, requiring the combined judgments of political and military leaders; decisions cannot be made according to abstract models poised to execute forces against predictable targets. Efforts to harmonize military criteria with political objectives may involve the redirection of resources and missions, a redirection that will impinge on traditional prerogatives and that will need a strong partnership between political and military authorities to be implemented effectively.

The recent integration of the functions of the joint strategic target-planning staff into the Joint Chiefs of Staff is one step toward better integration of military and political considerations in designing nuclear scenarios and a targeting strategy. Greater linkages between national command authorities and the Strategic Command are still needed. Decisions about what a potential aggressor "values most" and how operations could be kept within the confines of stated objectives need the active involvement of policymakers—not only U.S. officials but allied officials as well. Whether STRATCOM should be considered the center of expertise for deterring new security challenges, including biological and chemical weapons, is under evaluation. The remoteness of the Strategic Command from the world of policy, however, and its predilection for preferring the predictable over the complex make it ever less appropriate to manage future challenges.

The most important constraints on the credibility of nuclear options are political, stemming from a deeply embedded reluctance of policymakers to imagine a failure of deterrence. The experience of Desert Storm lent some urgency to articulating nuclear options in advance of crises. But this experience is more noteworthy for the opposition of President Bush and his senior advisers to give serious consideration to nuclear retaliation even against chemical attacks. Colin Powell said he was "unnerved" by the strike options developed by his joint staff and told them to destroy the papers.[47]

It is past time for decisionmakers to resolve some of the contradictions in U.S. doctrine, including the relevance of U.S. nuclear operations for weapons proliferation and regional conflict. The increasingly popular notion that U.S. strategy falls apart in the face of a third world nuclear or chemical adversary, for example, suggests that the architecture of U.S. nuclear deterrence is increasingly meaningless and, perhaps, needlessly high risk. In the haste to define nuclear threats and countermeasures, there has been scant opportunity for an adequate evaluation of the legacy of nuclear weapons for global security, let alone time to think about the dangers that these weapons posed and may still pose to their traditional possessors.

What are the lessons the established powers might derive from nuclear deterrence, from their different operational practices, and from their use of nuclear threat? Which among these lessons would we want other states to emulate? The long-standing consensus that nuclear weapons prevented war between the two superpowers and account for the stability of Europe after World War II has discouraged analysts from examining the dynamics of nuclear deterrence in detail.[48] The moderating influence of nuclear weapons is taken as creed and is borne out by one obvious empirical fact: the absence of war. Detailed accounts of episodes in which accidents or false information led to inadvertent escalation and the near use of nuclear weapons over the last four decades, however, suggest a far more complicated legacy. The extent to which it was sheer luck and not just strategy or the judiciousness of leaders that prevented war has not been adequately explored.[49] Until such questions can be answered, it will be difficult to undertake a redesign of the nuclear posture in a way that demonstrably contributes to security.

Notes

Chapter 1

1. Admiral Henry G. Chiles Jr., "Managing a Stable Strategic Drawdown," *Defense Issues*, vol. 10 (1995).

2. R. James Woolsey, testimony before the Senate Armed Services Committee, March 1995, cited in Loch K. Johnson, "Strategic Intelligence and Weapons Proliferation," *Monitor*, vol. 1 (Spring 1995), p. 5 (Center for International Trade and Security, University of Georgia).

3. Office of the Secretary of Defense, *Proliferation: Threat and Response* (Government Printing Office, 1997), p. iii.

4. As elaborated in a May 1997 White House document, *A National Security Strategy for a New Century*, pp. 6–7, "Unstable nations, internal conflicts or failed states may threaten to further destabilize regions where we have clear interests. . . . Some threats transcend national borders. These transnational threats, such as terrorism, the illegal drug trade, illicit arms trafficking, international organized crime, uncontrolled refugee migrations and environmental damage threaten American interests and citizens."

5. Bryan Bender, "Pentagon Found Ill-Prepared for Asymetric Warfare," *Defense Daily*, vol. 197 (October 8, 1997), p. 5.

6. William G. Hyland, "A Mediocre Record," *Foreign Policy*, vol. 101 (Winter 1995–96), pp. 69–74; Vincent A. Auger, "Seeking a 'Simplicity of Statement': The Search for a New U.S. Foreign Policy Doctrine," *National Security Studies Quarterly*, vol. 3 (Spring 1997), pp. 1–20; and Richard N. Haass, "Paradigm Lost," *Foreign Affairs*, vol. 74 (January 1995), pp. 43–58.

7. Thomas S. Kuhn, *The Structure of Scientific Revolutions,* 3d ed. (University of Chicago Press, 1996).

8. Quoted in Tyler Marshall, "Once Explosive, Arms Control Is No Longer a Hot Issue," *Los Angeles Times,* December 18, 1996, p. A2 (Washington edition).

9. See Mellman Group, *Public Attitudes on Nuclear Weapons: Presentation and Analysis of Findings for Committee on Nuclear Policy* (September 1997), p. 2; and Hank C. Jenkins-Smith, Kerry G. Herron, and Richard Barke, *Public Perspectives of Nuclear Weapons in the Post–Cold War Environment* (Albuquerque: Sandia National Laboratories, 1994).

10. A rich literature in political science theory analyzes the role of bureaucracies, interest groups, the presidency, or the Congress as powerful determinants of policy outcomes. Graham Allison's analysis of the Cuban missile crisis, *Essence of Decision,* is still the classic work about the influence of bureaucratic politics on foreign policy. According to this model, governments are anything but "unitary actors" reacting rationally to systemic forces. They are complex organizations replete with agencies that bring different interests, calculations, perceptions, and types of leader to bear on policy deliberations. Far from determining domestic outcomes, international events are only the organic matter that gets filtered and distorted through the rival prisms of different political actors. As Allison defines the behavior of governments, "The name of the game is politics: bargaining along regularized circuits among players positioned hierarchically." See Graham Allison, *Essence of Decision: Explaining the Cuban Missile Crisis* (Little Brown, 1971), p. 144.

11. I. M. Destler, Leslie H. Gelb, and Anthony Lake, *Our Own Worst Enemy: The Unmaking of American Foreign Policy* (Simon and Schuster, 1984), p. 13.

12. Curt Weldon, "Nuclear Terrorism," Nuclear Roundtable, Henry L. Stimson Center, October 24, 1997, p. 4.

13. Andrew F. Krepinevich, "The Quadrennial Defense Review and Military Transformation," *National Security Studies Quarterly,* vol. 3 (Winter 1997), pp. 27–36; Eliot Cohen, "Calling Mr. X," *New Republic,* January 19, 1998, pp. 17–19. Also, see National Defense Panel, *Transforming Defense: National Security in the 21st Century* (1997).

14. Office of the Secretary of Defense, *Report of the Quadrennial Defense Review* (Government Printing Office, 1997); Office of the Secretary of Defense, *Report on the Bottom Up Review* (Government Printing Office, 1993).

15. For further discussion of the way in which authority for nuclear operations is delegated, see Peter Feaver, *Guarding the Guardians: Civilian Control of Nuclear Weapons in the United States* (Cornell University Press, 1992); and Janne E. Nolan, *Guardians of the Arsenal: The Politics of Nuclear Strategy* (Basic Books, 1989).

16. For a theoretical discussion of the distinct patterns of authority for and influence over domestic and national security organizations, see Amy Zegart, "In Whose Interests? The Making of American National Security Agencies" (Ph.D. diss., Stanford University, 1996).

17. Robert Dahl, *Controlling Nuclear Weapons: Democracy versus Guardianship* (Syracuse University Press, 1985), pp. 7–8.

18. For further discussion, see introduction to Ashton B. Carter, John D. Steinbruner, and Charles A. Zraket, eds., *Managing Nuclear Operations* (Brookings, 1987), and chapters 2 and 3 in this study.

19. Russell E. Dougherty, "Psychological Climate of Nuclear Command," in Carter, Steinbruner, and Zraket, *Managing Nuclear Operations*, pp. 413–14.

20. Nolan, *Guardians of the Arsenal*, pp. 249, 252.

21. Dougherty, "Psychological Climate of Nuclear Command," p. 420.

22. Louis Henkin, "Foreign Affairs and the Constitution," *Foreign Affairs*, vol. 66 (Winter 1987–88), p. 298.

23. See National Conference of Catholic Bishops, "The Challenge of Peace: God's Promise and Our Response," May 3, 1983, imprinted by the United States Catholic Conference. For the Court's statement, see International Court of Justice Advisory Opinion on "Legality of the Use by a State of Nuclear Weapons in Armed Conflict," The Hague, July 8, 1996.

24. Douglas Berenson, "DOD Concedes Strategic Missile De-targeting Deal Is Easily Reversed," *Inside the Pentagon*, vol. 13 (May 29, 1997), p. 1.

25. See chapter 3 for further discussion; and R. Jeffrey Smith, "Clinton Directive Changes Strategy on Nuclear Arms: Centering on Deterrence, Officials Drop Terms for Long Atomic War," *Washington Post*, December 7, 1997, p. A1.

26. Senior NSC official, interview by author, March 1998. The details of START and other arms control initiatives are discussed further in chapter 2.

27. Smith, "Clinton Directive."

28. Congressional Budget Office, *The START Treaty and Beyond* (Government Printing Office, 1991), p. 16.

29. Chiles, "Managing a Stable Strategic Showdown," p. 1.

30. The John J. McCloy Round Table Discussion Series on the Elimination of Nuclear Weapons, Council on Foreign Relations, Washington, D.C. (ongoing as of May 1997); and the National Academy of Sciences, Committee on International Security and Arms Control, *The Future of U.S. Nuclear Weapons Policy* (National Academy Press, 1997). In addition to these groups, a prior study initiated by the Henry L. Stimson Center and chaired by General Andrew Goodpaster involved a number of conservatives and senior military officers, including Ambassador Paul Nitze (former chief arms negotiator), General Charles Horner (former commander of air force space command), and General William Burns (former Joint Chiefs representative for intermediate-range nuclear forces), to develop specific proposals for the phased elimination of nuclear weapons under international safeguards. See Henry L. Stimson Center, *An Evolving U.S. Nuclear Posture*, Report 19 (Washington, 1995). Many of these recommendations were later adopted by a group of fifty senior retired military officers, including General George Lee Butler, former commander of STRATCOM. See Generals George Lee Butler and Andrew J. Goodpaster, "Joint Statement on Reduction of Nuclear Weapons Arsenals: Declining Utility, Continuing Risks," December 4, 1996. See also chapters 3 and 5 of this study for further discussion.

31. See Baker Spring, "What the Pentagon's Nuclear Doctrine Review Should Say," *Heritage Foundation Backgrounder* 987, May 26, 1994; Andrew F. Krepinevich Jr., "Forging a Path to a Post-Nuclear U.S. Military," *Issues in Science and Tech-*

nology, vol. 13 (Spring 1997), pp. 79–84; and Robert G. Joseph and John F. Reichart, "Deterrence and Defense in a Nuclear, Biological and Chemical Environment," *Comparative Strategy* (January–March, 1997) (Center for Counter-Proliferation Research, Institute for National Security Studies, National Defense University).

32. For additional discussion of Butler's views, see R. Jeffrey Smith, "The Dissenter," *Washington Post Magazine,* December 7, 1997, p. 18.

33. "Back from the Nuclear Brink," *Washington Post,* December 11, 1997, p. A26.

34. Mellman Group, "Presentation and Analysis of Findings for the Committee on Nuclear Policy," cover memo, November 6, 1997, p. 5.

35. Smith, "Clinton Directive." The intricacies of planning, launch, and command authority are examined in detail by several analysts, including Paul Bracken, "Delegation of Nuclear Command Authority," in Carter, Steinbruner, and Zraket, *Managing Nuclear Operations,* pp. 352–72; Bruce G. Blair, *The Logic of Accidental Nuclear War* (Brookings, 1993); and Feaver, *Guarding the Guardians.*

36. Jeff Erlich, "Are Nuclear Arms Needed?" *Air Force Times,* March 1997, p. 7.

37. The significant literature of organizational theory identifies patterns of bureaucratic and political conflict according to the character, purpose, and resulting biases of organizations. Organizations are biased toward perpetuation of accepted routines and familiar mechanisms in a way that can act as a powerful deterrent to the recognition of institutional limitations and to the acceptance of innovations. In some areas of national security policy, the decades of protection from external oversight, the presumption of privacy accorded by secrecy and compartmentalization, and the unique status accorded to the "national command authority" may add additional disincentives. See chapter 2 for further discussion.

38. Dahl, *Controlling Nuclear Weapons,* pp. 7–8

39. Testimony of General George Lee Butler, Defense Policy Panel, and Department of Energy Defense Nuclear Facilities Panel of the House Committee on Armed Services, *Regional Threats and Defenses for the 1990s,* 102d Cong., 2d sess. (Government Printing Office, 1993), p. 252

40. Presentation by General George Lee Butler to the National Academy of Science, April 28, 1996.

Chapter 2

1. Cited in R. Jeffrey Smith, "U.S. Trims List of Targets in Soviet Union," *Washington Post,* July 21, 1991, p. A1.

2. For more detailed discussion of targeting criteria and other aspects of nuclear operations, see Carter, Steinbruner, and Zraket, *Managing Nuclear Operations,* especially Donald C. Latham and John J. Lane, "Management Issues,

Planning, Acquisition and Oversight," pp. 640-60. See also Blair, *The Logic of Accidental Nuclear War.*

3. The number of targets is cited in Bruce G. Blair, *Global Zero Alert for Nuclear Forces* (Brookings, 1995), p. 73. The SIOP is based on the national target list, which derives from, and is constantly updated with, intelligence about enemy capabilities and installations. For further discussion, see Leon Sloss, *Rethinking Nuclear Employment Policy* (Lawrence Livermore National Laboratory, Calif.: Center for Technical Studies on Security, Energy and Arms Control, January 25, 1991); and chapter 3 of this study.

4. Curtis Lemay, interview by John T. Bolen, U.S. Air Force Oral History Program, Interview 736, March 9, 1971, Maxwell Air Force Base, p. 33.

5. Desmond Ball, "The Development of the SIOP, 1960–1983," in *Strategic Nuclear Targeting,* edited by Desmond Ball and Jeffrey Richelson (Cornell University Press, 1986), p. 58.

6. Dougherty, "Psychological Climate of Nuclear Command," pp. 412, 413, 417.

7. Quoted in William Arkin, "How Much Isn't Enough?" paper prepared for the Center for Strategic and International Studies, September 17, 1992, p. 7.

8. Dougherty, "Psychological Climate of Nuclear Command," p. 418.

9. Peter Gray, "Briefing Book on U.S. Leadership and the Future of Nuclear Arsenals," Council for a Livable World Education Fund, Washington, September 1996, p. 5.

10. Senate Committee on Armed Services, *Inquiry into Satellite and Missile Programs: Hearings before the Preparedness Investigating Subcommittee,* 85th Cong., 1st and 2d sess. (Government Printing Office, 1958), pp. 1, 2.

11. For further discussion, see David Alan Rosenberg, "The Origins of Overkill: Nuclear Weapons and American Strategy 1945–1960," *International Security,* vol. 7 (Spring 1983), pp. 3–71.

12. For a detailed discussion of nuclear operations in Europe, see Catherine McArdle Kelleher, "NATO Nuclear Operations," in Carter, Steinbruner, and Zraket, *Managing Nuclear Operations,* pp. 445–69; and Ivo H. Daalder, *The Nature and Practice of Flexible Response: NATO Strategy and Theater Nuclear Forces since 1967* (Columbia University Press, 1991).

13. This number does not include theater nuclear forces—which were under the command of regional commanders in Europe (USCINNEUR), the Atlantic Command (CINCLANT), and the Pacific Command (CINCPAC)—or the nuclear capable forces that were part of NATO's allied command. For trends in the growth of strategic arsenals, see Committee on International Security and Arms Control, National Academy of Sciences, *The Future of U.S. Nuclear Weapons Policy* (National Academy Press, 1997), app. B, pp. 105–10.

14. Institute for Defense Analysis, "Weapons Systems Evaluation Group Report 50, Enclosure C," September 1960. Cited in Stephen Schwartz, ed., *Atomic Audit: The Costs and Consequences of U.S. Nuclear Weapons since 1940* (Brookings, 1998), p. 207. Major investments were made to improve the command system, especially during the Reagan administration, but this essential dilemma remains.

15. These arrangements were accompanied by elaborate efforts to ensure that the decision to launch forces would be protected against false warning or unauthorized acts. For a detailed discussion of safety measures, see Feaver, *Guarding the Guardians*; and Scott D. Sagan, *The Limits of Safety: Organizations, Accidents, and Nuclear Weapons* (Princeton University Press, 1993).

16. For extensive discussion of the dynamics of U.S. and Soviet command and control, see Blair, *The Logic of Accidental Nuclear War*, pp. 38–58.

17. Former JSTPS official, interview by author, August 1996.

18. Latham and Lane, "Management Issues," p. 642.

19. Ibid., p. 643.

20. Interview by author, August 1997.

21. Henry Rowen, "Formulating Strategic Doctrine," in *Report of the Commission on the Organization of the Government for the Conduct of Foreign Policy*, vol. 4 (Government Printing Office, 1975), app. K, pt. 3, p. 233.

22. Dougherty, "Psychological Climate of Nuclear Command," p. 420.

23. Former SAC commander, interview by author, August 1997.

24. Nolan, *Guardians of the Arsenal*, p. 254.

25. Ibid., p. 255.

26. General George Lee Butler, quoted in Smith, "The Dissenter," p. 44. For a more detailed account of presidential SIOP briefings, see Nolan, *Guardians of the Arsenal*, chap. 5.

27. Nolan, *Guardians of the Arsenal*, p. 261.

28. For further discussion of these and subsequent measures, see Graham T. Allison and others, *Avoiding Nuclear Anarchy: Containing the Threat of Loose Russian Nuclear Weapons and Fissile Material* (MIT Press, 1996); and Amy F. Woolf, "Nuclear Weapons in the Former Soviet Union: Location, Command, and Control," Congress Issue Brief 91144, November 27, 1996.

29. Two military participants in Cheney's review, interviews by author, August 1997.

30. Cited in David B. Ottaway and Steve Coll, "Trying to Unplug the War Machine," *Washington Post*, April 12, 1995, p. A1.

31. This observer claims that the greatest obstacle to achieving reductions in nuclear targeting earlier was the JSCP guidance, which "at the insistence of the civilian leadership in DoD, continued to call for targeting requirements that much of the cognizant military leadership thought excessive." Senior military official, interview by author, May 1997.

32. Former air force chief of staff, interview by author, August 1997.

33. Dougherty, "Psychological Climate of Nuclear Command," p. 412.

34. Former chairman of the Joint Chiefs, interview by author, October 1997.

35. Quoted in Hans Kristensen, "Targets of Opportunity: How Nuclear Planners Found New Targets for Old Weapons," *Bulletin of the Atomic Scientists*, vol. 53 (September–October 1997), pp. 22-28.

36. Kristensen, "Targets of Opportunity."

37. Interview by author, July 1997.

38. For further discussion of the Bush arms control legacy, see Hal Feiveson, ed., *The Nuclear Turning Point: A Blueprint for Deep Cuts and Dealerting of Nuclear Weapons* (Brookings, 1999).

39. See chapter 3; and Robert Bell, senior director for the National Security Council for defense policy and arms control, press briefing, White House, March 24, 1997.

40. Kristensen, "Targets of Opportunity."

Chapter 3

1. For further discussion of these measures, see Allison and others, *Avoiding Nuclear Anarchy;* and Woolf, "Nuclear Weapons in the Former Soviet Union."

2. For an illustrative presidential address on detargeting and related issues, see White House, Office of the Press Secretary, "President William Jefferson Clinton Address to the Nixon Center for Peace and Freedom Policy Conference," March 1, 1995.

3. White House, Office of the Press Secretary, "Strategic Stability and Nuclear Security," joint statement of Presidents Clinton and Yeltsin, September 28, 1994.

4. Krepinevich, "Forging a Path," pp. 80–81. He also quotes a conclusion of General Butler, STRATCOM commander, that some former economic targets in the U.S. operational plan "hardly warrant a conventional attack."

5. Ibid., p. 81.

6. In a statement praising Ukraine's progress in disarmament, Secretary of Defense William Cohen captured the essential message that the United States tried to impart to other countries about the dangers of nuclear weapons: "The people of Ukraine recognize that security comes from constructive alliances and not from nuclear weapons." News Briefing, *USIS Washington File,* May 1, 1997, p. 1.

7. The "negative security assurance" policy was articulated in June 1978 by Secretary of State Cyrus Vance: "The United States will not use nuclear weapons against any non-nuclear-weapons state party to the NPT [Nuclear Non-Proliferation Treaty] or any comparable internationally binding commitment not to acquire nuclear explosive devices, except in the case of an attack on the United States, its territories or armed forces, or its allies, by such a states allied to a nuclear weapon state or associated with a nuclear weapons state in carrying out or sustaining the attack. U.S. Arms Control and Disarmament Agency, *Documents on Disarmament, 1978* (Government Printing Office, 1979), p. 384.

8. National Defense Panel, *Transforming Defense: National Security in the 21st Century* (December 1997), p. 51. See also Krepinevich, "Forging a Path," pp. 79–84.

9. Les Aspin, "Three Propositions for a New Era Nuclear Policy," speech presented at the Massachusetts Institute of Technology, June 1, 1992.

10. For the latter, see Schwartz, ed., *Atomic Audit.*

11. For further discussion, see Senate Committee on Armed Services, *Briefing on the Results of the Nuclear Posture Review,* 103d Cong., 2d sess., (Government Printing Office, 1994), pp. 1–60.

12. The Nuclear Posture Review was codified in Presidential Review Directive 34, setting the mandate for a study intended to set the direction of U.S. nuclear policy for the following decade.

13. Quoted in Senate Committee on Armed Services, *Briefing on the Results of the Nuclear Posture Review,* p. 31.

14. Aspin, statement to the press, October 29, 1993.

15. NSC officials, interview by author, April 1997.

16. NPR participant, interview by author, June 1997.

17. In addition, Frank Miller, principal deputy assistant secretary and a veteran of several administrations' nuclear policy formulations, chaired the working group on strategy and deterrence and also the Executive Committee, which was to oversee the overall study. For an elaboration of the structure of the review, see Senate Committee on Armed Services, *Briefing on the Results of the Nuclear Posture Review,* charts 6 and 7.

18. Ottaway and Coll, "Trying to Unplug the War Machine," p. A1.

19. Ibid., p. A1.

20. Senior Pentagon officials and Washington defense correspondents, interviews by author, August–September 1996.

21. Former STRATCOM officer, interview by author, June 1994.

22. These views have been confirmed through interviews by author with senior military officers and through subsequent private statements by Owens in the fall of 1997 calling for unilateral cuts in U.S. nuclear forces well beyond START II.

23. Perhaps understandably in light of his responsibilities, Butler's public pronouncements as the commander of STRATCOM affirmed that START I levels of 4,700 weapons were the minimum level needed for deterrence in 1992 and postulated START II levels as the floor beneath which U.S. strategy would no longer be viable under the nuclear posture review. See Defense Policy Panel and Department of Energy Defense Nuclear Facilities Panel, *Regional Threats and Defenses for the 1990s,* p. 257.

24. Not least was the sudden ascendance of President Reagan's vision for a strategic defense initiative in 1983. Miller's critiques of "defense dominance" to replace traditional deterrence, an innovation he believed to be delusional and politically motivated, had won him a demotion in the early Reagan years. See Nolan, *Guardians of the Arsenal,* chaps. 1, 5.

25. A more jaundiced view of Miller's relationships with nuclear planners, expressed by a participant in the Nuclear Posture Review who was disappointed in the process, argues that there is a "bad incentive structure" for career civil servants when it comes to the challenges of policy innovation. "These officials have to survive after the end of an administration and depend on the good

will of their military colleagues. With the pace of promotions from Lieutenant Colonel to three or four star generals now taking less than ten years, it's no mystery why [career professionals] are reluctant to oppose even junior officers. They're coopted." Former senior military officer, interview by author, August 1996.

26. Senior Pentagon official, interview by author, September 1996.

27. Former Pentagon official, interview by author, August 1996.

28. Military participant in the review, interview by author, June 1996.

29. Former Pentagon official, interview by author, August 1996.

30. The logic underlying the need to shift doctrinal and targeting assumptions after the cold war are discussed in detail in Steve Fetter, "Nuclear Strategy and Targeting Doctrine," in Fieveson, ed., *Nuclear Turning Point*.

31. Several studies in the recent past describe force postures that deemphasize the need for alert forces and counterforce targeting in favor of smaller forces with greater survivability and operational transparency. See Jonathan Dean, "The Road Beyond START: How Far Should We Go?" consultation paper, The Atlantic Council of the United States (March 1997); Michael E. Brown, "Phased Nuclear Disarmament and U.S. Defense Policy," Occasional Paper 30 (Washington: Henry L. Stimson Center, October 1996); National Academy of Sciences, *The Future of U.S. Nuclear Weapons Policy*; and Blair, *Global Zero Alert*.

32. Several participants in the review, interviews by author, August– September 1996, February 1997, June 1997.

33. Former Pentagon official, interview by author, December 1996.

34. Military participant in the review, interview by author, June 1996.

35. Chiles, "Managing a Stable Strategic Drawdown," p. 3.

36. Interview by author, August 1997.

37. Former Pentagon military officer, interview by author, December 1996.

38. For a discussion of why minimum deterrence would lead to the "immoral" targeting of civilians, see, for example, Thomas C. Reed and Michael O. Wheeler, "The Role of Nuclear Weapons in the New World Order," draft report, December 1991, p. 28, and William Daugherty, Barbara Levi, and Frank von Hippel, "The Consequences of 'Limited' Nuclear Attacks on the United States," *International Security*, vol. 10 (Spring 1986), pp. 3–45.

39. Bill Gertz, "The New Nuclear Policy: Lead but Hedge," *Air Force Magazine*, January 1995, p. 36. Gertz emphasizes that "the real news of [the nuclear posture review] is what it did not change. . . . The NPR made no apparent shift in the underlying concept of deterrence," p. 35.

40. House Committee on Armed Services, *Regional Threats and Defenses for the 1990s*, p. 272; and Center for Security Policy, "Clinton's Reckless Nuclear Agenda Revealed?" Decision Brief 97-D 96 (July 12, 1997), p. 3.

41. Reed and Wheeler, "The Role of Nuclear Weapons."

42. William M. Arkin, "Agnosticism When Real Values Are Needed: Nuclear Policy in the Clinton Administration," *F.A.S. Public Interest Report*, vol. 47 (September/October 1994), p. 7. See also chapter 4 of this study.

43. Former Pentagon official, interview by author, August 1996.

44. John Deutch and Admiral Owens were exceptions. In the case of Deutch, however, it is widely perceived that he was interested mainly in finding savings from nuclear cuts and lost interest in force restructuring when it was demonstrated that the savings would be offset by higher up-front costs for dismantlement and related activities. State Department official, interview by author, September 1996.

45. R. Jeffrey Smith, "Clinton Decides to Retain Bush Nuclear Arms Policy," *Washington Post*, September 22, 1994, p. A1.

46. Pentagon official, interview by author, June 1996.

47. Ottaway and Coll, "Trying to Unplug the War Machine."

48. Steve Fetter, interview by author, December 1996.

49. Frank Miller, interview by author, March 1997.

50. Former Pentagon official, correspondence with author, February 1997.

51. Leo Mackay, interview by author, August 1996.

52. The letter was signed by Major General Larry Henry, air force acting deputy chief of staff for plans and operations, Lieutenant General John Tilelli, army operations deputy, Rear Admiral John Redd, navy assistant deputy chief of naval operations for plans, policy, and operations, and Brigadier General Thomas Wilkerson, marine corps acting operations deputy to the Joint Chiefs of Staff. See Elaine Grossman, "Four Services Sign Letter to Block Carter's Nuclear Posture Brief," *Inside the Air Force*, vol. 5 (April 29, 1994), pp. 1, 8–9.

53. Senate Committee on Armed Services, *Department of Defense Authorization for Appropriations for FY95 and the Future Years Defense Program*, August 20, 1994, pt. 1., 103d Cong., 2d sess. (Government Printing Office, 1994), p. 995.

54. The letter was signed by senators Conrad Burns (R-Mont.), Malcolm Wallop (R-Wyo.), Alan Simpson (R-Wyo.), and Dirk Kempthorne (R-Idaho). The full text is cited in Grossman, "Four Services Sign Letter," p. 9.

55. Review participants, interviews by author, 1996–97.

56. Former Deputy Secretary of Defense John Deutch, interview by author, February 1997.

57. Telephone interview by author, January 1997.

58. Steve Fetter, interview by author, June 1996.

59. Elaine Grossman, "At Last Minute, Nuclear Posture Review Backs 450–500 ICBMs—For Now," *Inside the Air Force*, vol. 5 (September 23, 1994), p. 10.

60. Ibid.

61. Gertz, "The New Nuclear Policy," p. 34.

62. Ibid.

63. Speech delivered by William J. Perry, Henry L. Stimson Center's 1994 Award for Public Service Ceremony, Decatur House, Washington, D.C., September 20, 1994.

64. Secretary of Defense William J. Perry, *Annual Report to the President and the Congress*, February 1995, p. 10. The Nuclear Posture Review also imposed requirements on the Department of Energy to maintain the viability of nuclear weapons without underground testing, including the ability to design and produce new warheads, a robust science and technology infrastructure, and

ways to ensure adequate supplies of tritium, which would require a new tritium plant.

65. Pentagon official, interview by author, July 1997.

66. Ottaway and Coll, "Trying to Unplug the War Machine." According to their account, a briefing presented by Carter and Perry to Pavel Grachev, the Russian defense minister, provoked unintended antagonism when an interpreter translated *lead* in the lead-and-hedge strategy as "dominate," and *hedge* as either "shrubbery" or "the ability to break out from treaty commitments." The more substantive reasons for opposition included Russian concerns about the renewed U.S. commitment to "hard-target-kill" targeting options and to preparations for prompt operations, including alert levels for missile forces.

67. Telephone interview by author, January 1997.

68. Under the hedge strategy and current legislation, the administration cannot move to START II levels until the agreement is ratified by the Russian Duma. The Defense Department had to reprogram funds to pay for a START I force beginning in fiscal year 1999. The costs of a hedge strategy will increase dramatically after fiscal year 2000, to more than $10 billion by 2003, including payment for platforms such as additional Trident C-4 submarines. See Elaine M. Grossman, "Russian Failure to Ratify START II Would Cost U.S. $10 Billion after FY-00," *Inside the Pentagon*, vol. 12 (April 25, 1996), p. 1.

69. National Defense Panel, *Transforming Defense: National Security in the 21st Century* (1997).

70. Stephen S. Rosenfeld, "Still on a Cold-War Footing," *Washington Post*, October 31, 1997, p. A25.

71. Smith, "Clinton Decides to Retain Bush Nuclear Arms Policy."

Chapter 4

1. In addition to the Nuclear Non-Proliferation Treaty, agreements include the Protocol for the Prohibition for the Use in War of Asphyxiating, Poisonous or other Gasses and of Bacteriological Methods of Warfare. This is known as the Geneva Protocol, which has 145 signatories. See June 17, 1925, 26 U.S. T 571, Department of State, *Treaties in Force 242*, 1985. The Geneva Protocol is bolstered by the Convention on the Prohibition of the Development, Production and Stockpiling of Bacteriological and Toxic Weapons and on Their Destruction, opened for signature on April 10, 1972, and entered into force in 1975; 26 U.S. T 538. Chemical weapons now fall under the Convention on the Prohibition of the Development, Production, Stockpiling and Use of Chemical Weapons and on Their Destruction, opened for signature January 13, 1993. See PrepCom document PC/CWC-S.R./12 (January 1996). Programs for biological and chemical development have been under way for many years in third world states, but efforts at international regulation (or to gather intelligence) on these capabilities was a very low foreign policy priority until the early 1990s.

2. Treaty on the Non-Proliferation of Nuclear Weapons, article 6. The full text of the treaty can be found in *Arms Control and Disarmament Agreements, Texts and Histories of Negotiations* (Government Printing Office, 1982), pp. 82–95.

3. As summarized by the director of the U.S. Arms Control and Disarmament Agency John Holum, under article 6, "the nuclear weapon states promise measures to reduce and eliminate their nuclear arsenals." Testimony before the Senate Foreign Relations Committee on the Second Strategic Arms Reduction Treaty, January 31, 1995, 104th Cong., 1st sess. (text available from the U.S. Arms Control and Disarmament Agency).

4. For further discussion, see Kristensen and Handler, *Changing Targets*.

5. Testimony of General Lee Butler, STRATCOM commander, February 1993, cited in ibid., p. 6.

6. Smith, "Clinton Directive."

7. U.S. Strategic Command, "Counterproliferation and the Silver Book," April 26, 1994, p. 3. (This report has been partially declassified and was released under the Freedom of Information Act.)

8. Blair, *Global Zero Alert*, p. 8.

9. Emphasis added. Senate Committee on Armed Services, *Hearings on the Department of Defense Authorization for Appropriations for FY 1995*, p. 979.

10. Nolan, *Guardians of the Arsenal*, p. 261.

11. Elaine Grossman, "Korea, Europe CINCs Object to STRATCOM Bid for Global Planning Role," *Inside the Air Force*, vol. 6 (March 18, 1994).

12. Defense Policy Panel and Department of Energy Defense Nuclear Facilities Panel, *Regional Threat and Defense Options for the 1990s*, pp. 275–76.

13. Kristensen and Handler, *Changing Targets*, p. 6.

14. Reed and Wheeler, "The Role of Nuclear Weapons in the New World Order."

15. Kristensen and Handler, *Changing Targets*, p. 6.

16. Joint Chiefs of Staff, Office of the Chairman, *Doctrine for Joint Nuclear Operations*, Joint Publication 3-12, April 1993.

17. Les Aspin, "An Approach to Sizing American Conventional Forces for the Post-Soviet Era: Four Illustrative Options" (Government Printing Office, 1992).

18. Aspin, "Three Propositions for a New Era Nuclear Policy," p. 2.

19. Richard Pipes, "Why the Soviet Union Thinks It Could Fight and Win a Nuclear War," in *U.S.-Soviet Relations in the Era of Detente* (Boulder, Colo.: Westview Press, 1981), p. 147.

20. Smith, "The Dissenter," p. 41.

21. Doug Bereuter, "U.S. Security Toward Rogue Regimes," *Hearings before the House Subcommittee on International Security, International Organizations and Human Rights*, 103d Cong., 2d sess. (Government Printing Office, 1994).

22. Jenkins-Smith, Herron, and Barke, *Public Perspectives of Nuclear Weapons*, p. 18.

23. Interview by author, May 1996.

24. See Samuel P. Huntington, "The Clash of Civilizations?" *Foreign Affairs*, vol. 72 (Summer 1993), pp. 22-49.

25. Anthony Lake, "From Containment to Enlargement," speech delivered at the Paul H. Nitze School of Advanced International Studies, Johns Hopkins University, Washington, D.C., September 21, 1993.

26. U.S. Department of Defense, "Quadrennial Defense Review," Section 2, "The Global Security Environment," May 19, 1997, p. 4.

27. Office of the Deputy Secretary of Defense, "Report on Nonproliferation and Counterproliferation Activities and Programs," May 1994, p. 1.

28. Rajiv Gandhi, letter to Prime Minister Shri Chandra Shekhar, February 9, 1991.

29. Senior National Security Council official, interview by author, July 1996.

30. In addition the report by Reed and Wheeler ("The Role of Nuclear Weapons in the New World Order"), the Pentagon was examining the role of small, low-yield nuclear devices against rogue countries. In April 1993 the Joint Chiefs reportedly approved the concept of limited nuclear wars using a "selective capability of being able to use lower-yield [nuclear] weapons." See David B. Ottaway and Steve Coll, "U.S. Focuses on Threat of Loose Nukes," *Washington Post,* April 10, 1995, p. A1. See also John Fleck, "Sandia Redesigns N-Bomb," *Albuquerque Journal,* September 22, 1995, p. A1.

31. For further discussion, see Paul I. Bernstein and Lewis A. Dunn, "Adapting Deterrence to the WMD Threat," in *Countering the Proliferation and Use of Weapons of Mass Destruction,* edited by Peter L. Hays, Vincent J. Jodoin, and Alan R. Van Tassee (McGraw-Hill, 1998), pp. 150–51.

32. An Israeli Air Force general, interview by author, March 1996.

33. "Mr. Perry's Backward Nuclear Policy," editorial, *New York Times,* March 24, 1994, p. A22.

34. National Security Council official, interview by author, May 1996.

35. White House, Office of the Press Secretary, "President William Jefferson Clinton Address to the Nixon Center."

36. Clinton speechwriter, interview by author, May 1996.

37. Department of State, Statement of Secretary of State Warren Christopher, April 5, 1995. Known as a negative security assurance, this statement builds on a long-standing U.S. policy that was articulated in June 1978 by then Secretary of State Cyrus Vance: "The United States will not use nuclear weapons against any non-nuclear-weapons state party to the NPT or any comparable internationally binding commitment not to acquire nuclear explosive devices, except in the case of an attack on the United States, its territories or armed forces, or its allies, by such a state allied to a nuclear weapon state, or associated with a nuclear weapon state in carrying out or sustaining the attack." U.S. Arms Control and Disarmament Agency, *Documents on Disarmament, 1978,* p. 384.

38. Quoted in George Bunn, "Expanding Nuclear Options: Is the U.S. Negating Its Non-Use Pledge?" *Arms Control Today,* vol. 26 (May–June 1996).

39. National Security Council official, interview by author, May 1996.

40. The Treaty for the Prohibition of Nuclear Weapons in Latin America (Treaty of Tlatelolco) was opened for signature in 1967 and now has twenty-seven Latin American and Caribbean contracting parties. Argentina, Chile, and Brazil became signatories in 1994. The United States is a party to two protocols to the treaty. The South Pacific Nuclear-Free Zone Treaty (Treaty of Raratonga) was opened for signature in 1985 and now has eleven contracting parties. The United States signed the treaty's three protocols on March 25, 1996.

41. Spurgeon M. Keeny Jr., "Nuclear Policy in Disarray," *Arms Control Today*, vol. 26 (April, 1996), p. 2.

42. Cited in Greg Mello, "New Bomb, No Mission," *Bulletin of Atomic Scientists*, vol. 53 (May–June 1997), p. 32.

43. Pentagon official, interview by author, June 1996.

44. Efforts to extend negative security assurances by formal agreement also sparked internal disputes. Ambassador Robert Gallucci encountered Pentagon resistance when he proposed extending a binding pledge to North Korea as part of the framework agreement to stop the Korean nuclear program, a pledge that had been granted to Ukraine.

45. Pentagon official, interview by author, June 1996.

46. State Department official, interview by author, August 1996.

47. National Security Council participants, interviews by author, January–March 1996.

48. The Pentagon expressed similar concerns about the South Pacific Nuclear-Free Zone Treaty, which was concluded during the Reagan administration. Motivated in large measure by the contamination of the island nations from decades of French nuclear tests, the agreement was crafted in consultation with individuals in the State Department and following the protocol signed by Russia and China (but not the United States). When asked in a congressional hearing six years later why the United States had still not signed, John Deutch, deputy secretary of defense, and Walter Slocombe, deputy undersecretary of defense for policy, focused on the U.S. requirement to "neither confirm nor deny" the presence of nuclear weapons on naval vessels: "The policy is to eliminate the capacity for American surface ships to carry nuclear weapons," although the option of keeping nuclear-armed cruise missiles on submarines is retained. "Given the vastly reduced role of nuclear weapons in the Navy under current circumstance," Slocombe continued, "there are still some reasons not simply to cast out [the policy of neither confirming or denying] automatically." Both officials stressed that the U.S. position was being reconsidered, and the United States signed the treaty's three protocols on March 25, 1996. See House Committee on Foreign Affairs, *Hearings on U.S. Nuclear Policy*, October 5, 1994, 103d Cong., 2nd sess. (Government Printing Office, 1995), p. 19.

49. The first quotation is from a senior appointee in the State Department, which was confirmed by Pentagon and State Department officials, interview by author, September 1996. The second quotation is from a National Security Council official, interview by author, August 1996.

50. Robert Bell, White House press briefing, April 11, 1996.

51. For a detailed discussion, see Bunn, "Expanding Nuclear Options," p. 7.

52. National Security Council official, interview by author, May 1996.

53. Heather Podlich, "Senate Panel Completes Hearings on Chemical Weapons Convention," *Arms Control Today*, vol. 26 (May 1996), p. 23.

54. Kevin Bacon, Pentagon press briefing, May 7, 1996, cited in Mello, "New Bomb, No Mission," p. 32.

55. The B-53 is an 8,900-pound, nine-megaton device developed to destroy cities; it was later adapted to attack underground targets, such as Soviet leadership bunkers. The B-61-mod-11 is a 1,200-pound version that enables it to be carried on bombers other than the B-52, has a range of yields that is far lower and more flexible, and is believed to be far more efficient in destroying targets. The B-61-11 program was the result of decisions taken around the time of the nuclear posture review and was endorsed by John Deutch, deputy secretary of defense, in February 1995. The development of earth-penetrating warheads (including the W-86 and W-85) was initiated during the Carter administration for the Pershing II missile and was revived in the Reagan administration to give ICBMs and air-launched cruise missiles the capability to destroy "deeply buried, superhard time-urgent targets" in the Soviet Union. These programs languished during the Bush administration as the cold war was ending, but interest has since been revived by the Clinton administration, beginning with a 1993 directive from the Pentagon's office of atomic energy to the air force to explore alternatives to the B-53. For further discussion, see Mello, "New Bomb, No Mission."

56. Pentagon officials, interviews by author, Wye Plantation, April 1996.

57. Director of the U.S. Arms Control and Disarmament Agency, statement before the U.N. Committee on Disarmament, January 1996, as cited in Mello, "New Bomb, No Mission," p. 32.

58. White House, Office of the Press Secretary, "Comprehensive Test Ban Treaty," Statement by President William Jefferson Clinton, April 11, 1995.

59. Thomas Dowler and Joseph Howard, "Countering the Threat of the Well-Armed Tyrant: A Modest Proposal for Small Nuclear Weapons," *Strategic Review* (Fall 1991), as cited in William Arkin, "Nuclear Junkies: Those Lovable Little Bombs," *Bulletin of Atomic Scientists*, vol. 49 (July 1993), p. 25.

60. Senior National Security Council official, interview by author, August 1996.

Chapter 5

1. Office of the Secretary of Defense, *Report on the Bottom Up Review*, p. 26.

2. Yegor T. Gaidar, "A View from Russia," *Foreign Policy*, no. 109 (Winter 1997–98), p. 64.

3. The threat of a militaristic Russia hostile to the West emerging in the place of a democratizing Russia seeking partnership has been an unchanging theme of the Clinton administration, even as it has sought to deepen cooperation with and assist Russia in the transition to democracy. Critics and media com-

mentators characterize the concurrent objectives as a nuclear hedge on their efforts to achieve cooperative threat reduction, an allegation dismissed by officials. See Steven Greenhouse, "U.S. to Russia: A Tougher Tone and a Shifting Glance," *New York Times*, March 21, 1994, p. A9; Henry Kissinger, "Beware: A Threat Abroad," *Newsweek*, vol. 127 (June 17, 1996), pp. 41–43; Dimitri K. Simes, "Russia: Still a Bear," *Washington Post*, July 9, 1996, p. A15; and Robert Kagan, "The New Russophobes Are Here," *Weekly Standard*, vol. 1 (July 1, 1996), pp. 25–27. The threat from China is described by some to be growing as a result of China's recent investments in missile forces, including a new mobile ICBM with the potential for carrying multiple, independently targetable, reentry vehicles (MIRVs). There are allegations that China was recently reintegrated into centralized nuclear attack plans. See Martin Sieff, "Missile Build-up in China Could Threaten US," *Washington Times*, November 12, 1993, p. A16; and Smith, "Clinton Directive." For discussion of the threat of other regional nuclear adversaries, see chapter 4.

4. Illustrative studies of proposals to vastly reduce or eliminate nuclear weapons include Steering Committee, Project on Eliminating Weapons of Mass Destruction, *Beyond the Nuclear Peril: The Year in Review and the Years Ahead*, Report 15 (Washington: Henry L. Stimson Center, January 1995); on the utility of nuclear weapons against third world states, see Joseph and Reichart, "Deterrence and Defense"; and Reed and Wheeler, "The Role of Nuclear Weapons." For a discussion of managed proliferation, see Bruce Bueno de Mesquita and William H. Riker, "An Assessment of the Merits of Selective Nuclear Proliferation," *Journal of Conflict Resolution*, vol. 26 (June 1982), pp. 283–306; and Stephen Van Evera, "Primed for Peace: Europe after the Cold War," *International Security*, vol. 15 (Winter 1990), p. 7.

5. *Congressional Record*, January 26, 1996, p. S462.

6. Sheila Foote, "Thurmond 'Concerned' about Nuclear Weapons Proposal," *Defense Daily*, vol. 194 (March 14, 1997), p. 1.

7. David Hoffman, "Yeltsin Approves Doctrine of Nuclear First Use If Attacked," *Washington Post*, May 10, 1997, p. A21.

8. For additional discussion, see James E. Goodby, "Can Strategic Partners Be Nuclear Rivals?" the Arthur and Frank Payne Distinguished Lectureship series, 1996–97, Center for International Security and Cooperation, Stanford University, February 1997. See also Melor Sturua, "NATO: From Truman via Yeltsin to Clinton," *Moscow Moskovskiy Komsomolets*, May 17, 1997 (FBIS-SOV-97-097, May 17, 1997); "LDPR Leader: Only Force Can Check NATO Enlargement," *Moscow Interfax*, May 8, 1997 (FBIS-SOV-97-128, May 8, 1997); "Russian, U.S. Ministers Agree on Some Issues; Not NATO," *Beijing Xinhua*, May 13, 1997 (FBIS-CHI-97-133, May 13, 1997); Pavel Anokhin, "Missiles without Targets. But What Are the Targets of the Sensation-Seekers?" *Moscow Rossiyskiye Vesti*, May 29, 1997 ("High-Ranking Officers Said to Welcome Yeltsin Initiative," FBIS-UMA-97-148, May 29, 1997).

9. The START III framework agreed to in Helsinki in March 1997 addresses the specific problem of the upload capabilities of MIRVed missiles as part of a

broader effort to improve the "transparency" of strategic inventories and to monitor the destruction of nuclear weapons, but no actions will be taken in this direction until Russia ratifies START II. See Nikolai N. Sokov, "Russia's Approach to Deep Reduction of Nuclear Weapons," *Washington Quarterly* (Summer 1997), pp. 107–14; and Rodney W. Jones and Nikolai N. Sokov, "After Helsinki, the Hard Work," *Bulletin of Atomic Scientists*, vol. 53 (July–August 1997), pp. 26–30.

10. General Eugene Habiger, "Deterrence in a New Security Environment," *Strategic Forum* 109 (Institute for National Strategic Studies, National Defense University, April 1997).

11. See Sokov, "Russia's Approach to Deep Reductions of Nuclear Weapons"; John D. Steinbruner, "Safety First: The Transformation of Nuclear Weapons Operations," paper prepared for the Common Security Forum, Fall 1993; and National Academy of Sciences, *The Future of U.S. Nuclear Weapons Policy*.

12. Fred C. Ikle, "Comrades in Arms: The Case for a Russian-American Defense Community," *National Interest*, no. 26 (Winter 1991), p. 25.

13. "Rodionov's Concerns about Nuclear Command and Control," Office of Russian and Eurasian Affairs, Central Intelligence Agency, reported in Bill Gertz, "Mishaps Put Russian Missiles in 'Combat Mode,'" *Washington Times*, May 12, 1997, p. A1.

14. Other concerns cited include the potential for severing links between political authorities and regional commands and submarines, wherein officers have the technical ability to launch weapons without authorization and the potential seizure of nuclear devices by members of separatist movements, such as Chechen leaders.

15. Council on Foreign Relations, *Nuclear Proliferation: Confronting the New Challenges*, Report of an Independent Task Force on Nuclear Proliferation (1995), p. xiii.

16. "Fifty Years from Trinity: Towards a New Consensus on Nuclear Weapons and U.S. Security," Report of the NGO Commission on the U.S. Nuclear Posture, Lawyers Alliance for World Security, the Committee for National Security, and the Washington Council on Non-Proliferation, September 22, 1994, p. 11.

17. The report also argues that the return to an alert posture ("assured regeneration") in crisis would impose high costs and thus discourage further reductions by adding to "the already significant costs of reduction." Larry D. Welch, "Chairman's Report," Study Group Paper, John J. McCloy Roundtable Discussion Series on the Elimination of Nuclear Weapons, Council on Foreign Relations, 1998, p. 10.

18. Illustrative examples of this point of view include George Quester and Victor Utgoff, "U.S. Arms Reductions and Nuclear Nonproliferation: The Counterproductive Possibilities," *Washington Quarterly*, vol. 16 (Winter 1993), p. 129; Michael Wheeler, "*Positive and Negative Security Assurances*," PRAC Paper 9, Center for International and Security Studies, University of Maryland, February 1994; and Strom Thurmond, "Unified Commanders and Operational Re-

quirements," in Senate Committee on Armed Services, *Defense Authorization for Appropriations for FY 1995 Hearing*, April 20, 1994, 103d Cong., 2d sess. (Government Printing Office, 1994).

19. Economic constraints have forced Russia to delay repairs in ground-based radars and to cut the deployment of satellites used for warning, while disputes with former Soviet states have led to more limited access to radar stations deployed on their territory. Latvia, for example, closed a radar station in September 1998, a move that the commander of Russia's strategic forces decried as damaging to Russia's already strained warning network. For further discussion, see Michael R. Gordon, "U.S. to Use Its Missile Warning System to Alert Russians to Launchings Worldwide," *New York Times*, September 2, 1998, p. A9.

20. For further discussion, see Walter Pincus, "Re-Read His Lips: Reduce Arms Now," *Washington Post*, October 11, 1998, p. C1.

21. *Congressional Record*, June 13, 1995, p. H5783; Woolf, "Nuclear Weapons in the Former Soviet Union."

22. Council on Foreign Relations and the Nixon Center for Peace and Freedom, "Arms Control and the US-Russian Relationship," 1996, p. 25.

23. An additional security challenge that is rarely addressed in official and congressional debates is the costs of handling, storing, and disposing of excess fissile material in a way that protects against proliferation risks and environmental damage, costs that could amount to hundreds of billions of dollars. For detailed discussion, see National Academy of Sciences, Committee on International Security and Arms Control, *Management and Disposition of Excess Weapons Plutonium* (National Academy Press, 1994).

24. Annual costs of maintaining the nuclear infrastructure are estimated to be $35 billion to $45 billion, compared to the few million appropriated for cooperative risk reduction. Among the examples of successful endeavors to reduce nuclear risks are programs undertaken by Sandia National Laboratories in Russia to assist in developing and implementing security procedures for nuclear facilities, which have achieved significant progress despite extremely limited resources. For further discussion, see Arian Pregenzer, "Reducing the Motivation for Proliferation by Supporting Regional Confidence Building," Cooperative Monitoring Center, Sandia National Laboratories, 1996.

25. Bunn, "Expanding Nuclear Options," p. 7.

26. Reed and Wheeler, introduction to "The Role of Nuclear Weapons in the New World Order," briefing by the chairman of the JSTPS/SAG Deterrence Study Group, October 10, 1991.

27. See, for example, Frank Gaffney, "Whistling Past Gallucci Gulch: Appeasement Will *Assure*—Not Prevent—Conflict with Pyongyang," Report 94-D103, Center for Security Policy, October 19, 1994; and Henry Sokolski, "The North Korea Understanding: Three Alternative Futures," paper presented at conference, North Korea after Kim Il Sung: Continuity or Change, Hoover Institution, February 27–28, 1996. U.S. policy toward China is coming under assault from both arms control advocates and those who see China as an emerging strategic threat; both favor harsher strictures against China for its continued missile and

nuclear technology exports, despite pledges to adhere to the Nuclear Non-Proliferation Treaty and the missile technology control regime.

28. Although they are often put into one category of mass destruction weapons, chemical and biological weapons pose different challenges. Chemical weapons are easier to produce and use but do not have the same lethality or persistent effects as biological weapons. Although crude biological devices can be easily assembled and have catastrophic effects, the risk they pose to the user inhibits their development. Biotechnologies are making the prospect of military applications of biological agents more likely. See Office of Technology Assessment, *Proliferation of Weapons of Mass Destruction: Assessing the Risks* (Government Printing Office, 1993); and John D. Steinbruner, "Biological Weapons: A Plague upon All Houses," *Foreign Policy*, no. 109 (Winter 1997–98), pp. 85–96.

29. For additional discussion, see Michael May and Roger D. Speed, "The Role of Nuclear Weapons in Regional Conflicts," Center for International Security and Arms Control, Stanford University, 1994.

30. According to one estimate, a ten-ton earth-penetrating warhead could inflict high rates of fallout and radiation over an area extending from one-half to two kilometers. See Dowler and Howard, "Countering the Threat of the Well-Armed Tyrant," p. 37.

31. Richard Betts, *Nuclear Blackmail, Nuclear Balance* (Brookings, 1987).

32. Estimates by General Gary Luck, commander in chief of U.S. forces in Korea, cited in David B. Ottaway and Steve Coll, "New Threats Create Doubt in U.S. Policy," *Washington Post*, April 13, 1995, p. A1.

33. Ibid.

34. Meeting sponsored by the Institute for Foreign Policy Analysis, September 1997.

35. U.S. Information Service, American Embassy, Moscow, press release, February 4, 1998.

36. Military participant in the Nuclear Posture Review, interview by author, January 1997.

37. One illustrative case is the political fallout from Robert McNamara's attempts to shift U.S. nuclear doctrine from the first-strike option to mutual assured destruction. Consider also the debacle that followed the Reagan administration's attempt at a unilateral reinterpretation of the Anti-Ballistic Missile Treaty in late 1985. See Nolan, *Guardians of the Arsenal*, chaps. 2 and 5.

38. Even with presidential leadership, moreover, there is no guarantee of success. The episodes of presidents supporting and failing to significantly alter the operational assumptions of nuclear doctrine date back to Truman. For more detailed discussion, see Nolan, *Guardians of the Arsenal*, chap. 5; and Feaver, *Guarding the Guardians*, chap. 6.

39. The large body of literature about presidents and presidential authority is illuminating both about the degree to which presidents are constrained by domestic circumstances and about how differences in leadership, in delegation of authority, and in other decisionmaking patterns affect outcomes. The leading theorist of presidential styles is Richard E. Neudstadt, whose *Presiden-*

tial Power and the Modern Presidents: The Politics of Leadership from Roosevelt to Reagan (Free Press, 1990), first published in 1960 and updated twice since, remains the classic work on the constraints presidents face in exercising leadership. For another excellent analysis of presidential styles, see Alexander L. George, *Presidential Decisionmaking in Foreign Policy: The Effective Use of Information and Advice* (Boulder, Colo.: Westview Press, 1980).

40. Former Bush White House adviser, interview by author, February 1997.

41. Former National Security Council official, interview by author, February 1997.

42. Ibid.

43. Henry Kissinger, *White House Years* (Little Brown, 1979).

44. Morton Halperin with Leo Mackay, "Terms of Reference," in Council on Foreign Relations, "Nuclear Policy Review," 1996.

45. Nolan, *Guardians of the Arsenal*, p. 13.

46. Interview with former air force chief of staff, July 1997.

47. Colin L. Powell with Joseph E. Persico, *My American Journey* (Random House, 1995), pp. 485–86.

48. Sagan, *The Limits of Safety*, cites John Lewis Gaddis and Robert Jervis as prominent examples of historians and political scientists advancing this basic logic. See John Lewis Gaddis, "The Long Peace: Elements of Stability in the Postwar International System," *International Security*, vol. 10 (Spring 1986), pp. 99–142; and Robert Jervis, *The Illogic of American Nuclear Strategy* (Cornell University Press, 1984). Kenneth Waltz, among others, expands the notion of the mediating influence of nuclear weapons to explain how the acquisition of nuclear weapons by new countries may enhance international stability. Since states are inherently rational, according to this logic, nuclear weapons will counter regional instability by making the prospect of war between antagonists far too dangerous. Kenneth Waltz, *The Spread of Nuclear Weapons: More May Be Better*, Adelphi Paper 171 (London: International Institute for Strategic Studies, 1981); and Kenneth Waltz with Scott Sagan, *The Spread of Nuclear Weapons: A Debate* (Norton, 1995).

49. As Sagan argues, "the underlying assumption that unites so many historians and political scientists on this issue is the belief that wars begin only when political leaders determine that war is in the interest of the state. These scholars are all following Clausewitz's famous maxim: 'War is a continuation of policy by other means.' War is seen as a rational tool, controlled and used by statesmen, to achieve important ends. Wars do not begin by accident." Sagan, *The Limits of Safety*, p. 262.

Index